Edward Arber, George Joye

An Apology Made by George Joy

Edward Arber, George Joye

An Apology Made by George Joy

ISBN/EAN: 9783744661072

Printed in Europe, USA, Canada, Australia, Japan

Cover: Foto ©ninafisch / pixelio.de

More available books at **www.hansebooks.com**

The English Scholar's Library of Old and Modern Works

GEORGE JOY

An
Apology made by George Joy
to satisfy, if it may be, W. TINDALE

1535

EDITED BY

EDWARD ARBER

F.S.A. ETC. LATE EXAMINER IN ENGLISH
LANGUAGE AND LITERATURE
TO THE UNIVERSITY OF
LONDON

WESTMINSTER
ARCHIBALD CONSTABLE AND CO.
1895

INTRODUCTION.

His *Apology* (here first reprinted from the only copy at present known, now in Cambridge University Library) passed immediately on to the list of the Forbidden Books of its time. It is, for us, one of the most important contributions to the earliest bibliography of the printed English *New Testament*: and as it carries that deeply interesting Story onward from the first editions of 1526, it may be regarded as a continuation of the documents embodied in the *Preface* to our photo-lithographic reprint of the fragment of the first Quarto of that year, republished by us on 15 Feb., 1871.

Mr. HENRY BRADSHAW, better known for his profound bibliographical knowledge of the First Century of printed literature, than even he is as Librarian to the University of Cambridge, has pointed out to us while preparing the present reprint, that the great "Apostle of England" always printed his name WILLYAM TINDALE: which, taken in conjunction with his only autograph extant, being, in Latin, W. TINDALUS, would seem to show that we should now spell his name WILLIAM TINDALE.

If the Reader would be on a level with the latest researches as to the first printed English Scriptures, confessedly one of the most difficult topics in the whole range of our Literature, he should consult, with this *Apology*, the following:

HENRY STEVENS, F.S.A.   *The Bibles in the Caxton Exhibition.* 1877.
FRANCIS FRY, F.S.A.   *Bibliographical Description of the Editions of the New Testament, Tyndale's version, in English.*   1878.
HENRY BRADSHAW, M.A.   Article on *GODFRIED VAN DER HAGHEN (G. H.), the publisher of TINDALE's own last edition of the New Testament in* 1534-5; in *The Bibliographer.*   No. 1.   Dec., 1881.

Although there is, undoubtedly, much more knowledge yet to be recovered in reference to this matter; the five works above indicated will furnish materials for a *true* acquaintance (so far as it can extend at present) of this most deeply interesting subject.

II.

Ur knowledge of the first Forbidden printed English Literature must chiefly come from three sources. The Texts themselves, which were printed on the Continent; what is said of them from the Outside, by prohibitions, confiscations, trials, &c.; and what is said of them from the Inside, by those who either had a hand in their production, or were acquainted with those who had.

Naturally, the contributions from the Inside are the most rare: as the Exiles would not show their hands in print, unless provoked to it by some quarrel. Thus we know of Roy and Barlow's printing at Strasburg, through Roy's quarrel with Tindale, as appears in the latter's *Parable of the Wicked Mammon*: and so now, but for this conflict over the word *Resurrectio*, we never should have got the glimpse behind the scenes which Joy here gives us.

He had been admitted, apparently for some three or four years, into the small inner circle of English exiles at Antwerp, whose lives were consecrated to the Reformation of their mother country. He calls Tindale, at *p.* 50,

My nowne felowe / my companion in lyke perel and persecucion / my familiare / so well knowne / vnto whom I committed solouingly my secretis / with whom gladly I went into the house of god.

Yet Tindale does not appear to have put much confidence in him, or to have acquainted him with his own plans.

If one might compare the English with the German Reformers, Tindale was our Luther. Joy, who accuses him of "chyding and brawling," at *p.* 32; says at *p.* 17, "He after his wont[ed] disdaynful maner agenst me fylipt them forth betwene his fynger and his thombe/ and what disdaynfull and obprobious wordis he gaue me," &c. Also, "Warned of me/but a fole and vnlearned as he bothe reputeth me and telleth yt me to my face/" *p.* 43. Frith was our Melancthon, "ientle and quyet and wel lerned," as Joy testifies at *p.* 33. And Joy was almost our Carlstadt.

It should be remembered that this text is as bitterly angry a retort as any Christian man could write. We may believe Joy in what he says about himself; but not so much in what he says about Tindale: whom, notwithstanding all, he unconsciously admires and thoroughly respects; though he is vexed at having been injured, as he thought, by so powerful an author.

Our motive for this reprint, however, is not the quarrel, interesting as that is; but the bibliographical information.

III.

His *Apology* teems with points of interest; the due elucidation of which would require a commentary three times its length. We shall best serve the reader by adding to it, in the very little space at our disposal, a few external facts that run together with information given us by JOY: whose life is already done to our hand, in COOPER's *Athen. Cantab.*, i. 114. Ed. 1858.

JOHN FOX, in the second edition of his *Actes and Monumentes*, printed under the title of the *Ecclesiastical History*, in 1570, prints the following as *A table of certain persons, abjured within the diocese of London*, as from the Register of that Bishop.

John Raimund, a Dutchman, 1528.

For causing fifteen hundred of TINDALE's *New Testaments* to be printed at Antwerp, and for bringing five hundred into England. *p.* 1184

John Row, Bookbinder, a Frenchman, 1531.

This man, for binding, buying, and dispersing of books inhibited, was enjoined, besides other penaunce, to go to Smithfield with his books tied about him, and to cast them into the fire, and there to abide till they were all burned to ashes. *p.* 1188.

Christopher, a Dutchman of Antwerp, 1531.

This man, for selling certain *New Testaments* in English, to JOHN ROW aforesaid, was put in prison at Westminster, and there died. *p.* 1189.

EDWARD HALLE, in his *Chronicle*, tells us the following stories:

Here is to be remembered, that at this present tyme, Willyam Tyndale had newly translated and imprinted the *Newe Testament* in Englishe, and [CUTHBERT TUNSTALL] the Bishop of London, not pleased with the translacion thereof, debated with hymself, how he might compasse and deuise, to destroye that false and erronious translacion (as he saied).

And so it happened that one Augustine Packyngton, a Mercer and Merchant of London, and of a greate honestie, the same time was in Andwarp, where the Bishope then was [? *Autumn of* 1529], and this Packyngton was a man that highly fauored William Tindale, but to the bishop vtterly shewed hymself to the contrary.

The bishop desirous to haue his purpose brought to passe, commoned of the *Newe Testamentes*, and how gladly he would bye them.

Packyngton then hearyng that he wished for, saied vnto the bishop, my Lorde, if it bee your pleasure, I can in this matter dooe more I dare saie, then moste of the Merchauntes of Englande that are here, for I knowe the Dutche men and straungiers, that haue bought theim of Tyndale, and haue them here to sell, so that if it be your lordshippes pleasure to paye for them, for otherwise I cannot come by them, but I must disburse money for theim, I will then assure you, to haue euery boke of them, that is imprinted and is here vnsolde.

The Bishop thinkyng that he had God by the toe, when in deede he had (as after he thought) the Deuell by the fiste, saied, gentle Master Packyngton, do your diligence and get them, and with all my harte I will paie for them, whatsoeuer thei cost you, for the bokes are erronious and naughtes and I entende surely to destroy theim all, and to burne them at Paules Crosse.

Augustine Packyngton came to Willyam Tyndale and saied, Willyam I knowe thou arte a poore man, and hast a hepe of *newe Testamentes*, and bokes by thee, for the whiche thou hast bothe indaungered thy frendes, and beggered thy self, and I haue now gotten thee a Merchaunt, whiche with ready money shall dispatche thee of all that thou hast, if you thynke it so proffitable for your self.

Who is the Merchant, said Tindale?

The bishoppe of London, saied Packyngton.

O that is because he will burne them, saied Tyndale.

Ye Mar[r]y, quod Packynton.

I am the gladder, said Tindale, for these two benefites shall come thereof: I shall get money of hym for these bokes, to bryng my self out of debt (and the whole worlde shall crie out vpon the burning of Goddes worde). And, the ouerplus of the money, that shall remain to me, shall make me more studious, to correct the said *Newe Testament*, and so newly to Imprint the same once again, and I trust the second will muche better like you, than euer did the first.

And so forward went the bargain, the bishop had the bokes, Packyngton had the thankes, and Tyndale had the money.

Afterward when mo *newe Testamentes* [*the second of the two Dutch editions of 5,000 copies in all, referred to at p.* 20] were Imprinted, thei came thicke and threfold into Englande, the bishop of London hearyng that still there were so many *Newe Testamentes* abroad [*in circulation*], sent for Augustyne Packyngton and saied vnto him: Sir how commeth this, that there are so many *Newe Testamentes* abrode, and you promised and assured me, that you had bought al?

Then said Packyngton, I promes you I bought all that then was to bee had: but I perceiue thei haue made more sence, and it will neuer bee better, as long as they haue the letters [*type*] and stampes [*matrices*]: therefore it wer best for your lordeshippe to bye the stampes to, and then are you sure.

The bishop smiled at hym, and saied, Well Packyngton well: and so ended this matter.

Shortly after, it fortuned one George Constantine, to be apprehended by sir Thomas More, whiche was then lorde Chauncellor of England, of suspicion of certain heresies. And this Constantine beyng with More, after diuerse examinacions of diuerse thynges, emong other Master More saied in this wise to Constantine.

Constantine I would haue thee plain with me, in one thyng that I will aske of thee, and I promes thee I will shewe thee fauor, in all the other thynges, whereof thou art accused to me. There is beyond the sea, Tyndale, Joye, and a great many mo of you. I knowe thei cannot liue without helpe, some sendeth them money and succoureth theim, and thy self beyng one of them, haddest parte thereof, and therefore knowest from whence it came. I praie thee who be thei that thus helpe them?

My lorde, quod Constantine, will you that I shall tell you the truthe?

Yea I praie thee quod my Lorde.

Mar[r]y I will quod Constantyne, truly, quod he, it is the Bishoppe of London that hath holpen vs, for he hath bestowed emong vs, a greate deale of money in *New Testamentes* to burne theim, and that hath and yet is our onely succoure and comfort.

Now by my trothe, quod More, I thynke euen the same, and I said so muche to the bishop, when he went about to bye them. [GEORGE CONSTANTINE *escaped from this imprisonment, and landed at Antwerp on* 6 *Dec.* 1531. *See Cott. MS. Galba B.* x. *fol.* 21.] [21 Hen. VII. fcl. 186. Ed. 1548.

Willyam Tindale/yet once more to the christen reader.

Hou shalt vnderstonde moost dere reader / when I had taken in hande to looke ouer the new testament agayne and to compare it with ye greke / and to mende whatsoeuer I coulde fynde amysse and had almost fynesshed ye laboure: George Joye secretly toke in hand to correct it also by what oc- casyon his conscyence knoweth: and pre- vented [anticipated] me / in so moche / yat his correcyon was prynted in great nombre / yer myne beganne.

When it was spyed and worde brought me; though it semed to dyuers other yat George Joye had not vsed ye offyce of an honest man / seinge he knew yat I was in correctynge it my selfe: nether dyd walke after ye rules of yat love and softenes which christ / and his disciples teache vs / how yat we shuld do nothynge of stryfe to moue debate / or of vayne glorie or of couetousnes. Yet I toke ye thinge in worth as I haue done dyuers other in tyme past / as one that haue moare experyence of ye nature and dysposicion of yat mannes com- plexion / and supposed that a lytle spyse of couetousnes and vayne glorie (two blynde gydes) had bene ye onlye cause yat moued him so to do / aboute whiche thynges I stryue with no man: and so followed after and corrected forth and caused this to be prynted / without surmyse or lokynge on his cor- rection.

But when the pryntynge of myne was almost fynesshed / one brought me a copie and shewed me so many places / insoche wyse altered that I was astonyed and wondered not a lytle what furye had dryuen him to make soche chaunge and to call it a *diligent correction*. For thorow out Mat. Mark and Luke perpetually: and ofte in the actees / and sometyme in John and also in the hebrues / where he fyndeth this worde *Resurreccion* / he chaungeth it into *ye lyfe after this lyfe* / or *verie lyfe* / and soche lyke / as one that abhorred the name of the resurreccion.

If that chaunge / to turne *resurreccion* into *lyfe after this lyfe* / be a dylygent correccion / then must my translacion be fautie in those places / and saynt Jeromes [*the Vulgate*] / and all ye translatours that euer I heard of in what tonge so euer it be / from ye apostles vnto this his dylygent correccyon (as he calleth it) which whither it be so or no / I permyt it to other mennes iudgementes.

But of this I chalenge George Joye / that he dyd not put his awne name thereto and call it rather his awne translacion: and that he playeth boo pepe / and in some of his bookes putteth in his name and tytle / and in some kepeth it out It is lawfull for who will / to translate and shew his mynde / although a thousand had translated before him. But it is not lawfull (thynketh me) ner yet expedyent for the edifienge of the vnitie of the fayth of christ / that whosoeuer will / shall by his awne auctoritie / take another mannes translacion and put oute and in and chaunge at pleasure / and call it a correction.

Moreover / ye shall vnderstonde that George Joye hath had of a longe tyme marvelouse ymaginacions about this worde *resurreccion* / yat it shuld be taken for the state of the soules after their departinge from their bodies / and hath also (though he hath been reasoned with ther of and desyred to cease) yet sowen his doctryne by secret lettres on that syde the see [*i.e., in England*] / and caused great division amonge ye brethren. In so muche that John Fryth beynge in preson in the towre of London / a lytle before his death / wrote yat we shuld warne him and desyer him to cease / and would have then wrytten against him / had I not withstonde him. Therto I have been sence informed yat no small nomber thorow his curiositie / vtterly denye the resurreccion of ye flesshe and bodye / affirminge yat the soule when she is departed / is the spirituall bodye of the resurreccion / and other resurreccion shall there none be. And I have talked with some of them my selfe / so doted in that folye / that it were as good perswade a post / as to plucke that madnes oute of their braynes. And of this all is George Joyes vnquyet curiosite ye whole occasion / whether he be of the sayde faccion also / or not / to that let him answer him selfe.

If George Joye wyll saye (as I wot well he will) that his chaunge / is the sence and meaninge of those scriptures. I answer it is soner sayde then proved : howbeit let other men iudge. But though it were ye verie meaninge of the scripture : yet if it were lawfull after his ensample to every man to playe boo pepe with the translacions that are before him / and to put oute ye wordes of ye text at his pleasure and to put in every where his meaninge : or what he thought the meaninge were / that were the next waye to stablyshe all heresyes and to destroye the grounde wherewith we shuld improve them. As for an ensample / when Christ sayth Jo. v. The tyme shall come in ye which all that are in the graves shall heare his voyce and shall come forth : they that have done good unto resurreccion of lyfe / or with the resurreccion of lyfe / and they that have done evell / vnto ye [resur]reccion or with the resurrection of damnacion. George Joyes correccion is / they that have done good shall come forth into the verie lyfe / and they that have done evell into the life of damnacion / thrustinge cleane out this worde *resurreccion.* Now by ye same auctorite / and with as good reason shall another come and saye of the rest of ye text / they yat are in ye sepulchres / shall here his voyce / that ye sence is / the soules of them that are in the sepulchres shall heare his voyce / and so put in his diligent correccion and mocke oute ye text / that it shall not make for ye resurreccion of the flesshe / which thinge also George Joyes correccion doth manyfestlye affirme. If the text be left vncorrupt / it will pourge hir selfe of all manner false gloses / how sotle soever they be fayned / as a sethinge pot casteth vp hir scome. But yf the false glose be made the text / diligentlye ouersene and correct / wherwith then shall we correcte false doctrine and defende Christes flocke from false opinions / and from ye wycked heresyes of raveninge of wolves ? In my mynde therfore a little vnfayned loue after the rules of Christ / is worth moche hie learninge / and single and sleyght vnder stondinge that edifieth in vnitie / is moche better then sotle curiosite / and mekenes better then bolde arrogancye and stondinge over muche in a mannes awne consayte.

Wherfore / concernynge the resurreccion / I protest before

xii [THE OCCASION OF JOY'S *APOLOGY*. W. Tindale.
Nov. 1534.

god and oure savioure Jesus Christ / and before the vniversall
congregacion that beleveth in him / that I beleve accordynge
to the open and manyfest scriptures and catholyck fayth/
that Christ is rysen agayne in ye flesshe which he receaved of
his mother ye blessed virgin marie / and bodye wherin he
dyed. And yat we shall all both good and bad ryse bothe
fleshe and bodye / and apere together before the iudgement
seat of christ / to receave every man accordynge to his dedes.
And that the bodyes of all that beleve and contynew in the
true fayth of christ / shalbe endewed with lyke immortalyte
and glorie as is ye bodye of christ.

And I protest before God and oure savioure Christ and all
that beleve in him / that I holde of ye soulest hat are departed as moche as maye be proved by manifest and open
scripture / and thinke the soules departed in the fayth of
Christ and loue of the lawe of God / to be in no worse case
than yee soul of Christ was from the tyme yat he delivered
his sprite vnto the handes of his father / vntyll the resurreccion of his bodye in glorie and immortalite. Neverthelater/
I confesse openly / yat I am not persuaded yat they be all
readie in the full glorie that Christ is in / or the elect angels
of god are in. Neither is it anye article of my fayth : for if
it so were / I se not but then the preachinge of the resurreccion of the fleshe were a thinge in vayne. Not withstondinge
yet I am readie to beleve it / if it maye be proved with open
scripture. And I have desyred George Joye to take open
textes that seme to make for yat purpose / as this is.

To daye thou shalt be with me in Paradise / to make
therof what he coulde / and to let his dreames aboute this
worde resurreccion goo. For I receave not in ye scripture ye
pryvat interpretacion of any mannes brayne / without open
testimony of eny scriptures agreinge thereto.

Moreover I take God (which alone seeth ye heart) to
recorde to my conscience / besechinge him yat my parte be
not in ye bloude of Christ / if I wrote of all yat I have wrytten
thorow oute all my boke / ought of an evell purpose / of envie
or malice to anye man / or to stere vp any false doctrine or
opinion in the churche of Christ / or to be autor of anye secte/
or to drawe disciples after me / or that I wolde be estemed or
had in pryce above the least chylde yat is borne / save onlye
of pitie and compassion I had and yet have on the blindnes of

my brethren and to bringe them vnto the knowledge of Christ/ and to make every one of them / if it were possible as perfect as an angell of heaven / and to wede oute all yat is not planted of our hevenly father / and to bring doune all that lyfteth vp it selfe agaynst the knowledge of the salvacion that is in ye bloude of Christ. Also / my parte be not in Christ / if myne heart be not to folowe and lyve accordinge as I teache / and also if myne heart wepe not night and daye for myne awne synne and other mennes indifferently / besechinge God to convert vs all / and to take his wrath from vs/ and to be mercifull as well to all other men / as to myne owne soule / caringe for the welth of the realme I was borne in / for the kinge and all that are therof / as a tender hearted mother wolde for hir only sonne.

As concerning all I have translated or other wise written/ I beseche all men to reade it for that purpose I wrote it: even to bringe them to the knowledge of the scripture. And as farre as the scripture approveth it / so farre to alowe it/ and if in any place the worde of god dysalow it / there to refuse it / as I do before oure savyour Christ and his congregacion. And where they fynde fautes / let them shew it me/ if they be nye / or wryte to me / if they be farre of : or wryte openly agaynst it and improve it / and I promyse them / if I shall perceave that there reasons conclude I will confesse myne ignoraunce openly.

Wherfore I beseche George Joye / ye and all other to / for to translate ye scripture for them selves / whether oute of the Greke / Latyn or Hebrue. Or (if they wyll nedes) as the fox in the grayes [*badger's*] hole challengeth it for his awne / so let them take my translacions and laboures / and chaunge and alter/ and correcte and corrupte at their pleasures / and call it their awne translacions / and put to their awne names and not to playe boo pepe after George Joyes maner. Which whethe he have done faythfully and truly / with soch reverence and feare as becommeth the worde of God / and with suche love and mekenes and affeccion to vnite and circumspexcion that the vngodlye have none occasion to rayle on the verite / as becometh ye servauntes of Christ / I referre it to the iudgement of them that knowe and love the truth. For this I protest / that I provoke not Joye ner any other man (but am prouoked / and that after the spytfullest maner of provokynge)

xiv [The Occasion of Joy's *Apology*.   W. Tindale.
                                         Nov. 1534.

to do sore agaynst my will and with sorow of harte that I
now do. But I neyther can nor will soffre of any man/that
he shall goo take my translacion and correct it without name/
and make soche chaungynge as I my selfe durst not do/as
I hope to have my parte in Christ/though the hole world
shulde be geven me for my laboure.

Finally that new Testament thus dylygently corrected/
besyde this so ofte puttinge out this word *resurreccion*/and I
wot not what other chaunge/for I have not yet reede it over
hath in the ende before the Table of the Epistles and
Gospelles this tytle:

      (Here endeth the new Testament dyly
    gentlye ouersene and correct and prin-
    ted now agayne at Andwarp/by me
    wydow of Christophell of Endho-
    uen. In the yere of oure Lord.
        A. M. D. xxxiiii.
          in August.)
    Which tytle (reader) I have here
    put in because by this thou
      shalt knowe the booke
        the better.
          Vale.

[The exact colophon of Joy's edition as in the copy No. 12,180 in
        the Grenville Collection is—

    ¶ Here endeth the new
    Testament diligently o꞉
    uersene and corrected/
    and prynted now agayn
    at Antwerpe/by me wy꞉
    dowe of Christoffel of
    Endouen Jn the ye꞉
    re of oure Lorde.
      M. C C C C.
    and. xxxiiij. in
      August.∴]

¶ An Apologye made by George
Joye to satisfye (if it maye be) w.
Tindale: to pourge and defende himself ageinst so many sclaunderouse
lyes fayned vpon him in Tindals vncharitable and vnsober Pystle so
well worthye to be prefixed for
the Reader to induce him into the vnderstanding of hys
new Testament diligently corrected and printed in the yeare
of oure lorde. M.
CCCCC. and
xxxiiij. in Nouember.

¶ I knowe and beleue that the bodyes of euery
dead man/shall ryse agayne at domes daye.

¶ Psalme cxx.
Lorde/delyuer me from lyinge lyppes/
and from a deceatfull tongue. Amen.·.

1 5 3 5

How we were once agreed.

Fter that w. Tyndale had put forth in prynt and thrusted his vncharitable pystle into many mennis handis / his frendis and myne vnderstanding that I had prepared my defence to pourge and clere my name whyche he had defamed and defiled / called vs togither to moue vs to a concorde and peace / where I shewed them my grete greif and sorowe / for that he shulde so falsely belye and sclaunder me of syche crymes which I neuer thought / spake / nor wrote / and of siche which I knowe wel his owne conscience doth testifye the contrarie / euen that I denied the Resurreccion of the bodie / but beleue it is constantly as himself : and this with other haynous crymes whiche he impingeth vnto me in his pistle / nether he nor no man els shall neuer proue : wherfore except Tin[dale]. (sayd I) wil reuoke the sclaunders fayned vpon me hym self / I wyl (as I am bounde) defende my fame and name / whiche there is nothyng to me more dere and leif And to be shorte aftir many wordis : It was thus thorowe the mocion of our frendis concluded for our agrement and peace : That ☜ The condycions of oure agrement. I shulde for my parte (a reason and rekenyng firste geuen why I translated this worde *Resurrectio* into the lyfe after this) permyt and leaue my translacion vnto the iugement of the lerned in christis chirche. And T[indale]. on his parte shuld cal agein his pistle into his hand / so to redresse it / reforme it / and correcke it from siche sclaunderous lyes as I was therwith offended and he coude not iustifye them / that I shulde be therwith wel contented / T[indale]. addyng with hys own mouthe that we shulde with one accorde in his next testament then in printing in the stede of this vncharitable pistle wherwith I was offended / salute the reders

with one comon salutacion to testifye our concorde: of these condicions we departed louyngly. Then after. v. or. vj. dayes I came to Tin[dale]. to se the correccion and reformacion of hys pistle / and he sayd he neuer thought of it sence / I prayd him to make yt redy shortely (for I longed sore to se it) and came agene to him after. v. or vj. dayes. Then he sayd it was so wryten that I coude not rede it: and I sayd I was wel aquainted with his hande and shulde rede it wel ynough: but he wolde not let me se it. I came agene the thirde tyme desyring him to se it / but then had he bethought him of this cauyllacion contrary to the condicions of our agrement / that he wolde firste se my reasons and wryte agenst them ere I shulde se this his reformacion and reuocacion. Then thought I / syth my parte and reasons be put into the iugement of the lerned / T[indale]. ought not to write agenst them tyl their iugement be done / no nor yet then nether / syth he is content before these men to stonde to their iugement / and not to contende any more of thys mater withe me. yet I came agene the fourthe tyme / and to be shorte: he persisted in his laste purpose and wolde fyrste se my reasons and wryte agenst them and then leaue the mater to the iugement of Doctour Barnes and of his felowe called Hijpinus pastour of. s. nicholas parisshe in Hambourg / adding that he wolde reuoke that euer he wrote that I shulde denye the resurreccion. Then I· tolde one of the men that was present at the condicions of our agrement all this mater: and wrote vnto the other these answers that I had: so ofte seking vpon T[indale]. to be at peace and to stande to hys promyse / desyering them al to moue him and aduyse him to holde his promyse / or els / if he wolde not / them not to blame me thoughe I defende my selfe and clere my fame whiche he hath thus falsely aud vncharitably denigrated / deformed / and hurte. But in conclusion I perceyued that T[indale]. was half ashamed to reuoke according to his promyse al that he coude not iustifye by me / and with whiche I was so offended. wherfore sythe he wolde not kepe promyse / I am compelled to answere here now for my selfe: which I desier euery indifferent reder to iuge indifferently.

[margin: ¶ Tindal first breaketh hys promyse.]

And **now** first of all / because thou shalt se more clerely (good reder) what moued T[indale]. thus to belye me: to rage and rayle vpon me / and what is T[indale's]. opinion and doctrine as concerning the state of the soulis departed / and also that he affirmed it constantly and defended the same vnto my face when I resoned agenst him more then once or twyse and proued him the contrary by the scriptures: mouyng him to reuoke his errour (which doctryne to confute and put it oute of some mennis headis / my conscience compelled of the truthe of goddis worde caused me to englysshe thys worde *Resurrectio* the lyfe aftir this) haue here his own wordis in his answere to. m. Moris seconde boke.

More. *And when M. More proueth that the saintis be in heuen in glory with christe alredy sayng. If god be their God / they be in heuen: for he is not the God of the deade.* lxxii. leif the seconde syde.

Tindal Here saith Tin[dale]. *that Morestealeth awaye christis argument where with he proueth the Resurreccion / that Abraham and all sayntis shuld ryse again and not that their soulis were in heuen: which doctrine was not yet in the worlde / and with that doctryne he taketh awaye the resurreccion quyte and maketh Christis argument of none effecte. For when christe allegeth the scripture that god is the God of Abraham / and addeth to that god is not the god of the dead / but of the lyuing: and so proueth that Abraham muste ryse agayne / I denye christis argument, et cetera.*

Joye. Here is it manifest that T[indale]. vnderstondeth not this place of scripture / nether knoweth whither cristis argument tendeth / nor yet the Saduceis opinion: and therfore no meruel though he geueth not this worde *Resurrectio* ther his proper significacion / of which ignorance this his errour springeth God so suffring vs to fal standing to miche in our own consaightis / thynking our self so highly lerned / and to translate and write al thingis so exquisitely and perfaitly that no man is able ether to do it better or to correck our workis: whose argument is this. If the soulis of the faithful were in heuen / there shulde be no resurreccion of their bodies / whiche inconuenience to avoide / he laith them down to slepe out of heuen as do the Anabaptists tyl domes daye / but here I meruell that Tin[dale]. is so sclenderly lerned in the forme of arguyng that he se not howe his antecedence may be true and consequence false: seyng that

¶ The confutacion of Tyndals opinion.

¶ Tindals argument.

¶ Th[e]anabaptistys opinion off the soulis departed.

the contrary of his consequence is necessary / that is to weit /
^{1 corinthio. 15} there shalbe the resurreccion of the flesshe: Paule
thus prouing it. If Christ be preached to haue rysen / how
^{Tyndals argu-} happeneth that some of you saie thee is no resur-
^{ment is proued}
^{false.} reccion? As who shuld thus argew / Christe our
head is rysen: wherfore yt must nedes folowe that his bodye
which is his chirche shall ryse ageyn. For wherfore shuld
the beyng in heuen of the soulis of Peter and Paule and of
all saintis / let the resurreccion of their bodies more then the
being in heuen of Christis soule those iij. dayes did let his
resurreccion? Tin[dale]. wil saye: They be al redy in ioye /
and therfore there nedeth no resurreccion. And I saye / so
was christis spirit and yet he rose agayn. And I denye
Tin[dale's]. argument / For were they in neuer so greate ioye /
yet must their bodies ryse agayn / or els he wil make christe
^{Mat. 5} a lyer and his doctryne false. Heuen and erthe shal
soner passe away then one iote of goddis worde shal passe
vnfulfilled. The verite hath sayd it and wryten it / concluding
that our bodies shal ryse agein: wherfore ther can no con-
dicionall antecedence of T[indale]. nor yet of any angel in
heuen make this conclusion false.

But let vs examen the text / and se the Saduceis opinion /
vnto the whyche Christe answereth so directly and so
^{The Saduceis} confuteth yt vtterly. The Saduceis / as wryteth
^{opinion.} that aunciaunt historiograph Josephus beinge
himself a iew / in his. xviij. boke the. ij. ca. sayd that the
^{acto. 23} soule of man was mortal and dyed with the
^{¶ Paule de-} bodie: and Paule confirming the same to be their
^{clareth the sa-}
^{duceis opinion.} opinion / addeth that thei said ther were nether
spirits nor angels: so that to saye there is nether spirit /
(spirit properly is the soule departed) nor aungel / is as
miche to saye as the soule is mortall / and no lyfe to be
aftir this: and the Saduceis in denying the lyfe aftir this /
denied by the same denye but onely those two: that is /
bothe spirit and angell: for if they had denyed by that
worde *Resurrectio* the generall Resurrection to in that place /
so had thei denied thre distincte thingis: but Paule addyng /
Pharisei autem vtraque confitentur / but the pharises graunt them
bothe two / declareth manifestly that thei denyed but onely
two thingis that is to saye bothe spirit and angell: for aftir
this present life tyl domes daye there is no lyfe of eny

creature but of these two creatures spirits and aungels. And if by this worde *Resurrectio* Paule had vnderstonden as T[indale's]. doth the resurrection of the flesshe / he wolde not haue sayd / the pharyses graunt them bothe / but all thre. For this worde *vtraque* as euery latyne man knoweth / is spoken but of two thingis only: but as for this my mynde I leaue it vnto the iugement of the lerned. And nowe shall I proue yt by christis owne answer / that the Saduceis in those places of Math. Mark. and Luke / denied that there mat. 22 mar. 12 is any lyfe aftir this: and so nether to be spirit nor luc. 20. angel / whiche is as miche to saye as towching the soule / it to be mortall. For yf it shuld lyue aftir the departing / thei thought to haue had taken christe in this trappe with their question of those. vij. brethren / that thei now being all a lyue aftir their dethe / shuld haue al seuen togither that one wyfe at once; for thei sayd that al these. vij. had hir here. But christe answerde them directly accordyng to their opinion: and not aftir Tin[dale's]. opinion of this worde *resurrectio* / telling them that thei erred being ignorant of the scriptures and also of the power of god / whiche pow[e]r christe Io. 5. 12 declareth to consist in the preseruing the dead a 1 ioan. 5 lyue / for because out of god the father and christe the sone / being that vere lyfe / all lyfe floweth / ye and that into the dead: whiche power to confirme into the confutacion of their opinion and their own confusion: he alleged these scriptures exodi. iij. But first he tolde them of the present state of the soulis departed / saynge that in the tother lyfe aftir this they nether marye / nor ar maried / but thei ar as the aungels of god in heuen.

Tindal And yet saith Tindal *this doctryne was not then in the worlde / and what is done with the soulis departed* In his exposition of. S. Ihon (*the scripture make no mencion / but it is a secrete* (saith Pystle. he) *layd vp in gods tresury.*

Joye. It is verely a depe secrete to him that is ignorant [of] so many playne scriptures whiche I shall here aftir brynge in prouyng their state in heuen. Here is also to be noted that christe in describing their present state / saith in the present tence. Thei mary not nor ar maryed / but ar lyke aungels / ye egall vnto aungels / and the sonnes of god saith Luke cap. xx. But yet yf Tindal wyll saye that the present tence is here taken for the future / and playe boo

pepe withe the tencis as he englissheth *resuscitantur* shal
mar. 12. ryse agen / and not are reuiued or resuscited / yet
must I aske hym whether that the children of that lyfe
luc. 20. and worthy that worlde (as Luke calleth them)
be not now more lyke aungels then they shalbe aftir the
resurreccion of their bodies? me thinketh that in thys
poynt / that they nether marye nor are maryed: aungels
and the spirits be now bothe a lyke: and the chyldren of the
lyfe or the worlde where now the blessed lyue with Christe /
are now more lyke aungels then they shalbe aftir the resurrection of their bodyes / for now they ar substances incor-
poral / immortall / and intellectuall / and so be aungels: but
then they shalbe bodely substances hauyng very flesshe and
bones which the aungels neuer had nor neuer shall haue.

But nowe let vs heare the scryptures wherwith christe
The text is confuteth their opinion and proueth the same thynge
her[e]expended that the saduceis denyed. Crist considering what
[i.e., ex-
pounded]. thing thei denied / sayd vnto them. *De resurrectione
vero mortuorum / non legistis quod vobis dictum est a deo / qui ait.
Ego sum deus Abraham. &c* That is to saye. As concernyng the
lyfe of them that be dead haue ye not red what is tolde you of
god saying: I am the God of Abraham / the god of Isaac /
and the god of Jacob: God is not the God of the deade / but
of the lyuinge. By this argument: god is the god of the
lyuing and not of the dead: God is the god of Abraham
Isaac and Jacob *ergo* Abraham Isaac and Jacob are a lyue:
christe concludeth planely / nothing els but that there is a lyfe
aftir this wheryn the soulis departed lyue / whiche conclusion
sith it is directly made ageynst the Saduces opinion / it must
nedis folow that thei denyed in this place that thinge whiche
christe proued / for christe was not so vncircumspecte to
proue one thing / they denying another / or els they myght
haue well obiected saying: Syr what is this answere to our
question? we aske the whose wyfe shall she be at the general
resurreccion of their bodyes? and thou answerest vs nothyng
els nor prouest vs any thing els with this scripture but that
there is a lyf after this wheryn the soulis departed nowe lyue:
and so to be both spirits and angels for that thei be lyke
aungels: If the Saduces here had denyed cheifely and
principally / by that worde *Resurrectio* the general resurreccion /
criste wolde haue proued it then by scriptures / as well as he
here proued them the lyfe of spirits separated from their

bodyes / and christe rendering the cause of his argument to
confirme the same and to declare the powr of god in so preseruing the dead a lyue saith *Omnes enim illi viuunt* / all men
lyue in him / or by hym. Also it is to be noted ^{luc. 20.}
diligently how that saynt Marke for the inducyng ^{mar. 12.}
of that autorite of Moses / setteth before the thing that yt
proueth in these wordis saying. *Ceterum de mortuis quod resuscitantur non legistis in libro Mosi. &c.* that is to saye. But as
touching the dead / that thei ar resuscited or they ar all redy
alyue (he saith not that they shalbe alyue or shall ryse agayne
as [Tindale]. in hys diligent last correccion turneth the
present [t]ence into the future : and the verbe passiue into a
neuter to stablissh his errour thus corrupting the text. And
lyke wyse he plaith with the verbe in Luke and in Marke he
englissheth the verbe of the preter tence *resurrexerint* / for the
future. So fayne wolde he wrest the wordis from their natyue
sence to serue for hys errour) haue ye not red in exodo what
Moses saith &c ? so that he induceth the autorite to proue
that they ar a lyue / and nothing lesse then to proue the
resurreccion of the flesshe. I wounder wherfore T[indale].
flittith from the text in these places. Here maye euery man
se / that this worde *Resurrectio* in this place / as in dyuerse
other places of scripture is taken for the lyfe aftir ^{Resurrectio}
this wheryn the soules now lyue tyl the resurreccion ^{hath two significations}
of their bodies as testifyeth Joan: And Tin[dale]. not ^{apo. 20.}
knowyng this significacion or not willing to se it / is gretely
to blame to write and so belye and sclaunder me sayng : That
for because I thus geuing the worde in his place his very
significacion / I do denye the resurreccion of the flesshe: which
I neuer doubted of but beleue it as constantly as he / I haue
preached and taught it / and so interpreted it where it so signifyeth and confesse it openly as euery man maye se that read
my workis / and as Tindals own conscience testifyeth the same.
For thoughe this place proueth not directly the resurreccion
of the bodies yet are there many places moo that proue it
clerely : as doth all the. xv. chapter of the first Pystle to the
Corin. where I englisshe it Resurreccion / and in the article
of our Credo : but in John / and in the. xj. cap. to the
Hebrwes where the worde signifyeth the lyfe of the spirits
departed / there I englissh it as the very worde signifyeth to
put the reder out of doubt and to make it clere lest he be

10 *A rekeninge is gyuen of my translation.* [27 Feb. 1535. G. Joye.

seduced and erre with Tind[ale]. beleuyng that the soulis slepe out of heuen : when sleape in scripture is properly and onely vnderstanden of the bodye which shal be awaked and ryse ageyne.

For I did translate thys worde *Resurrectio* in to the lyfe aftir <small>For two causes</small> thys/in certayne placis/for these two causes <small>is this worde *Resurrectio*</small> principally. First because the latyn worde/besidis <small>so translated.</small> that it signifieth in other places the Resurreccion of the bodye/yet in these it signifieth the lyfe of the spirits or <small>mat. 22</small> soulis departed as christis answere vnto the Saduceis/ <small>apo. 10</small> and John declare. Secondaryly/because that agenst the Anabaptistis false opinion/and agenst their errour whom Erasmus reproueth in hys exposicion of the Credo which saye the resurreccion of the soules to be this: that is to weet/ when thei shalbe called out of their preuey lurking places/ in whiche they had ben hyd from the tyme of their departyng vnto the resurreccion of their bodies/because (I saye) that agenste these erroneouse opinions/these places thus truely translated make so myche and so planely/that at thys worde *Resurrectio* the lyfe of the spiritis aftir this/their false opinion falleth and is vtterly condempned.

And if Tin[dale]. wolde loke beter vpon his booke and <small>Here it is come</small> folow not so miche his owne witte/he shulde fynde <small>to the grunde of one cause</small> that the hebrew worde which comonly is translated <small>*Surgo* to ryse.</small> into this verbe *Surgo*/the same some tyme saynt <small>*Maneo* to abyde or endure.</small> Jerome translated into *Maneo*/as in Isaye. *Verbum domini manet in eternum*/The worde of the Lorde endureth for euer/some tyme into theise verbis *sto* or *consto*/ as Isaye xlvj. And some tyme into theis verbis *Pono/constituo/ excito/facio stare in vita/vel seruo in vita* as in exo. cap. ix. of Pharao. *Et perfecto ideo posui te/vel excitaui te/seruaui te in vita/vel feci et stare/superstitem te volui esse plagis meis : vt ostendam in te fortitudinem meam &c.* that is to saye : Doutlesse or verely for this cause yet haue I set and constitute the or stered the vp/preserued the alyue to receyue my plages to declare my strength vpon the and to shewe that my name myght be knowne thorowte all the worlde : of the which <small>*Resurrectio* hath more significations then one.</small> verbe there cometh *Surrectio* and so *Resurrectio* whose rote and original sith it hath these so many dyuerse significacions/it must nedis folow that the nowne diriuyed oute therof haue as many/and so to signifye

that permanent and verye lyfe or the preseruing of them
styll a lyue / which significacion agreeth in all these placis of
these thre euangelistis / for thei all tel one and the same
storye. If T[indale]. will englisshe thys verbe *Resurgo* euery
where to ryse agayne in bodye / so shal he translate it falsely /
corruppe the text and bringe the reder in to no small errour /
as once did one preacher in a sermon / expownyng this verse
of the first psalm. *Ideo non resurgent impij in iudicio &c.*
englysshing yt thus: wherfore the vngodly shal not ryse
agayn in the iugement. wherat many were offended and
astonied / and some beleued that the vngodly shulde not ryse
agen at the generall iugement. which worde in that place
Philip melanchton / Martyne Bucere / Conradus Pellicanus /
zwinglius / Campensis / (men of greter knowleg / higher lerning / and more excellent iugement in holy scripture / in the
hebrew / greke and latyne then Tindal is or euer lykely to be)
translate it into these verbis: *consistunt / constant / perstant /
durant / viuunt*: rendering the verse thus. *Ideo non constant non
consistunt non durant / or non viuunt impii in iudicio &c.* that is
to saye the vngodlye abyde not / nor endure / nor lyue in the
company of the iust at the iugement: whether it be in the
generall or partic[u]lare iugement of euery soule departed / as
Rabbi Kimhy cyted of Bucere vpon that same verse taketh
Judicium in that place: Also Bartholomeus Vesthemerus
gathering out of the lerned mennis workis / in hys boke en-
titled *Collectanea communium troporum* / the dyuerse significacions of wordis / and the comon phrasis in the scripture:
declareth in the. iij. c. leif / in how many places this worde
Resurrectio is taken for the ferme permanent lyfe of the soulis
now departed: And Henrichus Bullyngerus / a man of grete
lerning and greter iugement both in the scriptures and the
tongues consenteth with me in the significacion of this worde
Resurrectio in these placis. Many wordis in dyuerse places of
the scripture haue diuerse / ye some contrari significacions:
which thyng if it be not diligently obserued of the translatour
translatinge one for a nother / he may sone erre and corrupt
the text into the grete perel of the reder. I am sure that
T[indale]. wil not euery where englisshe this worde *Benedico*
a lyke / as to blesse: for in some placis it signifieth to curse /
nor yet englesshe *pectum* synne / for in some placis it signifieth
the cowe or calfe offred vp for synne / and so the selfe sacrifice

offred vp for the synne / and the expiacion and clensing or purgacion from synne / as is christe hym selfe so called. But here wil Tin[dale]. let grete scorne that I being so vnlerned in the hebrewe and other tongues (as I am in very dede) shuld take vpon me to poynt him to this marke whyche ether of ignorance he sawe not / or els of a selfe wyll and froward mynde wolde not se yt.

Furthermore he findeth himself sore aggreued for that I haue so englysshed this worde *Resurrectio* in the. xj. chap. to heb. ii the hebrews in thys place. Some men were racked / and yet refused they to be redemed or delyuered / to the[e]ntent they might haue *potiorem resurrectionem* / saith the text : which T[indale]. englissheth a beter resurreccion : where it is playn that he englissheth it falsely / for sith he taketh here Resurreccion for the resurreccion of the flesshe : and this comparison is here betwene two resurreccions only / it must nedis folow that aftir T[indale]. there shuld be two resurreccions of our bodyes / of the which one is beter than the t[he]other : and these men so stretched and racked hauing experience of the worse resurreccion despysed the delyuerance to obtayne the beter. Here may ye se in what absurdytes and errours Tin[dale]. wrappeth himself for falsely translating thys worde *Resurrectio* in this place : wherfore according to his owne desier in the ende of hys first new testament desyering all that be able to mende that at was amysse in it and to geue the wordis (where he did it not himself) their right significacions : for he confesseth euen there that hys first translacion was a thinge borne before the tyme / rude and imperfit / rather begun then fynisshed / not yet hauing her right shape. This I saye hys owne desyer and confession and my conscience so compelled me and caused me where I sawe siche notable fautes to mende them / lest so many false bokis thruste into mennis handis might ether staye the reader or els seduce him into any errour. Therefore (I saye) I englisshe it thus / that thei mought receyue rather the beter lyfe : for the comparison consisteth betwene this lyfe / of whiche thei were werie / and the tother beter lyfe aftir this which thei so feruently desiered that they refused to be delyuered from their paynes. And euen in the next lyne before T[indale]. himself / magry his tethe : was compelled so to englysshe the same worde callyng yt lyfe / and not the resurreccion. wherby thou mayst se (good reader) of what stomake and mynde he wryteth agenst me. Let euery man loke in his first translacion : and there shal he read this text. *Mulieres acceperunt ex resurrectione mortuos suos* thus englysshed of himself. The wemen receyued their dead to lyfe ageyne. Lo here resurrection aftir T[indale]. signifyeth lyfe / and not the generall resurreccion : *ergo* T[indale]. aborreth this worde resurreccion and denyeth the resurreccion of the flesshe / these be his arguments ageinst me / wherwith (if he thinketh them so stronge) I do here snare and hold him faste / tyl he be able to loose him selfe. But yet I neuer red that / *ex* / shulde signifye / *ad* / as to translate *ex resurrectione* to lyfe / but rather from that lyfe. Also in this we differ here : for he calleth resurreccion the present lyfe of this worlde / which is no lyfe in comparison to the tother / and I cal it the lyf of the tother worlde wherin the blessed soulis lyue with criste tyl domes daye : and ther aftir euer more with their bodies to. But yet in his last newe testament so diligently corrected and compared wyth the greke / because he wolde varie and swarue fro my englysshing (ye from the trueth of the worde) he goyth aboute *per ambages* with a longe circumlocution / sayng raysed from dethe to lyfe agen : lo here *ex resurrectione* signifieth raysed vnto this lyfe agen / he had leuer thus play bo peep with. ij. wordis / turning *ex* into *ad* / and the nowne into a participle / and the very lyfe of the spirits separated into the dedly shadow of this worlde / then to say the trueth wyth me. Here maye ye se what shiftis this man maketh to discorde from me : ye rather from the trueth.

But let vs returne to Tin[dale]. his answere to M. More in the sayd place and se with what faithfulnes and reuerence he allegeth Paule. There he saith that Paulis argument is this / If ther be no resurreccion / we be of al wretches the most miserablest Here may ye se how T[indale]. runneth ryot of his own wit falsely belying Paule hauing no respecte vnto his book / nor yet dew reuerence vnto holy scriptures alleging them / It wolde haue wel becomen as grete a clerke as he is / first to haue turned to Paulis argument and loked more diligently whyther Paule had so knytte it togither / and not to haue coupled paulis consequence with an antecedence of his own ymaginacion / For this is Paulis argument. If we haue but in thys lyfe

Tindal is confuted.

1. corinthio. 15.

Tindal belieth paule.

onely oure hope fastened in christe / so were we miserablest of al men. He saith not If ther were no resurreccion / for so myght his antecedence be true and his consequence false: for admitted that as T[indale]. allegeth him / there were no resurreccion / yet foloweth it not that the electe nowe departed beinge (as now at laste he is compelled to graunt) in no worse case then christis spirit was from his deth tyl he rose agen / be most miserable of al men: for they that be yet a lyue / and they that be dead and not receyued into Abrahams bosom but in hel in tormentis be miche more miserable. But what saith T[indale]. to his own argument: for Paul made it not / verely euen thus.

Tindal *Nay Paule thou art vnlerned / Go to m. More and lerne a new waye. We be not most miserable thoughe we ryse not agene / for oure soulis go to heuen as sone as we be dead.*

Joye. This saith Tin[dale]. yroniously in a mok as though it were false / that oure soulis as sone as we be dead shulde go to heuen.

Tindal *And ar there in as grete ioye as Christ that is rysen agayne.*

Joye. In heuen dare I saye that thei be: ye and that in ioye / if they dye in the lorde / but whether in as grete ioye as christ himselfe / let More and T[indale]. dispute it.

Tindal *And I meruel* saith T[indale]. *that Paule had not counforted the Thessalonians wyth that doctryne / if he had wist it / that the soulis of their dead had bene in ioye as* he *dyd wyth the resurreccion that their dead should ryse agen.*

Joye. Neuer meruel at it Tindale / for Paule thought this present consolacion sufficient and could haue counforted them then with many mo / as with this of Christ. Joan. v. that who so here my worde and beleue in hym that hath sent me / hath lyfe euerlastinge and shall not come into condempnacion / but is passed ouer from dethe to lyfe. whiche consolacion because in that place and at that tyme Paule spake it not: is it a good argument that ther was non[e] siche? ye must beware (syr) how ye argew *a negatiuis* / for siche kynde of arguments be the worste and feblest that ye can make. It is a naughty argument / Paule dyd not comfort them with that doctrine / but with another as good / *ergo* that doctrine was false or was not in the world? ye may not iuge Paule as ignoraunt as you be in it / because he did not then

and there expresse it for in other places he declareth and
techeth that doctrine plenteously ynoughe.
  Now reade Tinda[le]. wordis in hys answere to M. Moris
fourth boke / and loke whether he graunteth not Cxij. lief the
playnly that the soulis sleap tyll domes daye / and seconde syde.
whether he calleth not the doctryne that they shulde lyue
euer : heythen and fleshly doctryne of the Philosophers
ioyned wyth the popis doctrine. And agayn in the .cxviij.
leif where vnto he remitted the reader in his table Cxviii. leif.
withe thys sentence / Soulis sleap / belying Christe and hys
Apostles saynge that they taughte non[e]other / And yet bothe
there in his answers and in his exposition vpon Johns Pystle
apon this text. And now lytle chyldren abyde in him / that
when he shall apeare. &c. He sayth yt is a depe secrete layd
vp in gods tresury And yet a lytle before vpon thys text.
And he is the satisfaccion &c. He bryngeth in Tindals wordes
Paule tellynge a longe tale in hys sleap (yf Tin[dale's]. them selfe.
doctryne be trew) and maketh Paule at laste to confesse that
he himself with other sayntis be in heuen / contrary to hys
own saynge / read the. xvj. lyne the fyrste syde of the. xij.
leif of the exposicyon of that text. And he is the satisfaccion
&c. And ther shalt thou se how Tindals wordis fight agenst
them selfe. Finally yf yt be so depe a secrete / no scripture
to make mencion of their state / I wounder what made Tindale
so bolde to saye and to wryte yt to / that thei sleap / and that
thei be not in heuen : and now at last to thinke thei be in no
worse case then was cristis spirit aftir his dethe vntil his
resurreccion. Aftir I had sene theise places and known
Tindals erroneouse opinion I resoned wyth hym as we walked
togither in the feeld more then once or twyse : bryngyng
ageynst him siche textis as me thought / proued playnely
agenst hym / as when christe answerde the theif hangyng by
his crosse saying. This daye thou shalt be with Luc. 23
me in paradyse. where I sayd It is manifest that if christe
had that daye commended hys spirit into hys fathers handis
in heuen (as he dyd indeed) and promysed that the spirit of
the theif shuld be with his spirit (for their bodies were not
togither) it must nedys folow that hys spirit was with paradyse is
cristis spirit in heuen. And to expresse the place taken for heuen
more playnly christe added saying / In paradyse / 2 cor. 12.
which is not els then in heuen. whych one autorite albe it / it had

bene sufficient for any mane that wolde haue admytted and receyued the sengle and playn veryte of cristis worde / yet I brought forthe christes wordis agayn describing the state of the faithful and vnfaithful aftir this lyfe / saying. Math. viij. I tell you verely that many shal come from the east and west and shal sit down to eat with Abraham Isaac and Jacob in the kyngdom of heuen / that is to saye / shalbe associated vnto Abraham and Isaac to be parte takers of their ioye and fruicyon in heuen / but the chyldren of the kyngdom of the deuyl shalbe cast forth into extreme derknesses where shalbe wepinge and gnasshing of tethe. This sitting downe at <small>Abrahams bosom.</small> table with Abraham / is not els but Abrahams bosome into which all that resembled Abraham in faith / aftir their departinge were receyued / as ye maye se of Lazarus. Luke. xvj. where the state of the electe and of the reprobated immediatly after their deth is described / th[e]electe to be borne of aungels into Abrahams bosome as was Lazarus / and the reprobated to be caste into hell into tormentis wyth <small>2. cor. 5 Erthy tabernacle / oure corruptible bodye. Heuenly tabernacle / is that ioye and gloriouse presence of God.</small> the ryche gloton. Then alleged I Paule saying : For we knowe that yf oure erthye tabernacle where in we dwell were destroyed / yet haue we a perpetual mansion not made with handis / in heuen : of these mansions all redy prepared of christe yt is wryten. Joan. xiiij. And at last Paule affirmeth that to be absent from the bodye / is to be present with god / saying. we haue confydence and aproue thys to be beter / that is to weit / to be absent from the bodye and to be present wyth god / which saying is spoken of the state of soulis now beyng with <small>Sleap is onely appropriated to the bodyes.</small> god / absent frome theyr bodyes yet a sleape in the erthe tyll thei be awaked and raised vp at the general iugement. Unto this pertayneth his sayingis also <small>Phi. 1.</small> vnto the Philippians / affirming that dethe is to himself more aduauntage then here to lyue : and therfore he desired to be losed from his bodye that he might be with criste his life : and this state to be miche beter then the lyfe <small>apo 14</small> of this worlde. Then I alleged John in the Apocalipse describing the states bothe of the dampned and also of the blessed that dye in the lorde hence forthe : which sith they be blessed from their dethe forth / it must nedis folow that <small>apo. 20.</small> thei be in blysse in heuen. And John repetyng the same state describyng it almost withe the same wordis saith those soulis were alyue and raigned with crist. M. yere &c. and calleth that lyfe of the soulis /*primam resurrec-* *tionem* / the first resurreccion : and hym blessed and holy which hath his parte in the fyrste resurreccion : here is it playn that this worde *Resurrectio* is not euery where taken a lyke as T[indale]. saith / and John describeth the state of the seconde resurreccion immediatly in the same cap. and calleth the state of the dampned the seconde dethe by whiche correlatiuis calling it the first resurreccion in respecte of the seconde / and those antithesis and puttyng one contrary agenst another euery reader maye gather whiche is the first lyf / and the firste dethe / whiche is the seconde dethe and seconde resurreccion.

_{The first resurreccion, is the lyf of the soulis.}

But these playn testimonyes of the scripture wolde take no place with Tindal / for he wrested and writeth them contrary to his own doctryne out of their proper and pure sence with fayned gloses to shift and seke holes / he aftir his wont[ed] disdaynful maner agenst me fylipt them forth betwene hys fynger and his thombe / and what disdaynfull and obprobrious wordis he gaue me for so resoning agenst hym I wyll not now reherce / lest I shuld minysshe the good opinion that some men haue in him.

Also ther is a playne descripcion of the state where vnto the soulis departed in crist he ar receyued Hebr. xij. ye ar not come vnto the hill Sinai which none might touche : but ye are come vnto the mounte zion the cite of the lyuing god / the heuenly Jerusalem / and vnto the innumerable company of aungels vnto the congregacion of our former first begoten fathers writen togither in heuen / and to god the iuge of al men / and vnto the spiritis of the pure iuste and vnto Jesus criste the mediatour of the newe couenant euen vnto the bespreigned bloude. Here is yt playne / that in this heuenly Jerusalem ar now the congregacion of our former fathers and the spirites of the iuste men / for aftir the generall resurreccion / this congregacion shalbe no spiritis / but the company of very men hauyng flesshe and bone / whiche the spiritis haue not : crist sayng to his disciples fele and touche me / for a spyrit hath nether flesshe nor bones.

But at laste I remember that I made hym thys reason / saynge. Syr ye knowe that christe is our head / _{1. cor. 15} and we his members / and altogither hys bodye / ye knowe also that christe is the firste frutis / and fore leader of them that sleap / Then I argewed thus / The bodye must nedis ^{ioan. 14 and. 17} folow the head / and whother the head went thither must the bodye folow (for crist optayned of his father that wheresoeuer he shuld be / there shulde his faithful be with him to se his glorie) but christis spirit departed slept not oute of heuen / but wente into the fathers handis in heuen / wherfore euen so shall ours aftir our dethe / if we dye his membres and in the lorde:

This reason did so byght Tindal / and stoke so faste vpon hym that he coude not shake it of / but is now at laste (thanked be god) constrayned to saye with me in hys goodly
Tindal   godly pistle agenst me / *that I thynke* (he dare not yet constantly affyrme it) *the soulis departed in the faith of crist to be in no worse case then the soule of criste was from the tyme he delyuered his spirit into the handis of his father vntyll the resurreccion of hys bodye.*

Joye. Here maye euery reader se / that though he thinketh now other wyse then he hathe wryten in so many placis / and now thynketh the very same that I euer affirmed and obiected agenste him / yet had he leuer ageinst his owne conscience thus enuyously withe so many spightfull lyes and sclaunders vnto my perpetuall infamy / hauyng no respecte vnto the sclaunders and hurte mynistred vnto the congregacion of Christe / nor yet to the gaudye and reioyse of our aduersaries / to haue wryten agenst me then to refrayned his penne and aknowleged hys errour. So prowd and arrogant are they that stonde so hyghly in their own consayght and false opinion / pertinatly to defende it though thei se it right false / rather then thei wolde seme conuicted especially of any simple and one that apereth not so wel lerned as thei be them selues.

The Apologye and answere, &c.

ut let vs now here Tindals vncharitable pistle set before hys newe Testament thus tytled.

Tindal *Vylliam Tindal / yet once more to the Christen Reader.* [*p.* ix.]

Joye. Tindale shulde haue goten hym more honesty / and lesse shame / yf he had writen once lesse to the reader.

Tindal *Thou shalt vnderstonde (most dere reader) when I had taken in hande to loke ouer the newe testament agayn / and to compare it with the greke / and to mende what so euer I coude fynde amysse and had almost fynesshed the laboure.* [*p.* ix.]

Joye. It was but loked ouer in deed nothinge performing his so large promyses added in the later ende of his first translacion to the reader / and I wounder how he coude compare yt with greke sith himselfe is not so exquysitely sene thereyn.

Tindal *George Joye secretly toke in hand to correct it also / by what occasyon his conscyence knoweth: and preuented me / in so moch / that his correccion was printed in greate noumbre / yer myne beganne. When it was spyed and worde brought me / though it semed to dyuers other that George Joye had not vsed the offyce off an honest man / seynge he knewe that I was in correctynge it my selfe: nether dyd walke aftir the rules of the loue and softenes which Christe and hys disciples teache vs / howe that we shulde do nothynge of stryfe to moue debate / or of vayne glorie / or of couetousnes. yet I toke the thinge in worth as I have done dyuers other in tymes past as one that haue more experience off the nature and disposicion off that mannes complexyon / and · supposed that a lytle spyse off couetousnes and vayne glorye / (two blynde goydes) had bene the onlye cause that moued him so to do / aboute which thinges I striue with no man: and so folowed aftir and corrected forth and caused this to be printed without surmyse or lokynge on hys correctyon.* [*p.* ix.]

Joye. Lo good Reder / here mayst thou se of what nature

and complexion T[indale]. is so sodenly fyercely and boldely
<small>☾ *Nolite iudi-*
care vt non
iudicemini</small> to choppe in to any mannis conscience and so to
vsurpe and preuent the office of god in iugment
which is onely the enseer and sercher of herte and mynde.
Thys godly man / iugeth and noteth me vaynglorious e curiouse
and couetouse / and al for correcking a false copie of the
testament that thei mought be the trwelyer printed agen / and
so not so many false bokis solde into the realme [*England*] to
the hurt and deceyt of the byers and reders of them. I cor-
reked but the false copye wherby and aftir whyche the printer
dyd sette his boke and correcked the same himself in the presse.

But I shall now playnly and sengly (for the trowth knoweth
no fucated polesshed and paynted oracion) declare vnto euery
man / wherof / howe / and by whom I was moued and desyered
to correcke this false copie that shulde els haue brought
forth mo then two thousand falser boke more then euer
englond had before.

First / thou shalt knowe that Tindal aboute. viij. or. ix.
yere a goo translated and printed the new testament in a mean
great volume / but yet wyth oute Kalender / concordances in the
margent / and table in th[e]ende. And a non aftir the d[e]wche
men gote a copye and printed it agen in a small volume
adding the kalendare in the begynning / concordances in the
margent / and the table in th[e]ende. But yet / for that they
had no englisshe man to correcke the setting / thei themselue
hauyng not the knowlege of our tongue / were compelled to
make many mo fautes then were in the copye / and so corrupted the boke that the simple reder might ofte tymes be
taryed and steek.

Aftir this thei printed it agein also without a correctour in
a greatter letter and volume with the figures in th[e]apocalipse
whiche were therfore miche falser then their firste.

when these two pryntes (there were of them bothe
aboute v. thousand bokis printed) were al soulde more
then a twelue moneth agoo [*i.e.*, *before February*, 1534] /
Tind ale]. was pricked forthe to take the testament in hande /
to print it and correcke it as he professeth and promyseth
to do in the later ende of his first translacion. But
T[indale]. prolonged and differred so necessary a thing and
so iust desyers of many men. In so miche that in the
mean ceason / the dewch men prynted it agen the thyrde

tyme [*in the Summer of* 1534] in a small volume lyke their firste
prynt/but miche more false then euer it was before. And yet
was T[indale]. here called vpon agen/seyng there were so
many false printed bokis stil put forth and bought vp so fast
(for now was ther geuen thanked be god a lytel space to breath
and reste vnto christis chirche aftir so longe and greuouse
persecucion for reading the bokes) But yet before this thyrd
tyme of printing the boke/the printer desiered me to correcke
it. And I sayd It were wel done (if ye printed them agene)
to make them truer/and not to deceiue our nacion with any
mo false bokis/neuertheles I suppose that T[indale]. himself wil put it forth more perfait and newly corrected/
which if he do/yours shalbe naught set by nor neuer solde.
This not withstanding yet thei printed them [*in the Summer
of* 1534] and that most false and aboute. ij. M. bokis/and had
shortly solde them all.

Al this longe while T[indale]. slept/for nothing came from
him as farre as I coude perceiue.

Then the dewche began to printe them [*in August*, 1534]
the fowrth tyme because thei sawe no man els goyng
aboute them/and aftir thei had printed the first leif which
copye another englissh man had correcked to them/thei
came to me and desiered me to correcke them their copie/
whom I answered as before/that if T[indale]. amende it with
so gret diligence as he promysethe/yours wilbe neuer solde.
yisse quod thei/for if he prynte. ij. m. and we as many/what
is so litle a noumber for all englond? and we wil sel ours beter
cheape/and therfore we doubt not of the sale: so that I perceyued well and was suer/that whether I had correcked theyr
copye or not/thei had gone forth with their worke and had geuen
vs. ij. m. mo bokis falselyer printed then euer we had before.

Then I thus considred with myself: englond hath ynowe
and to many false testaments and is now likely to haue
many more: ye and that whether T[indale]. correck his or
no/yet shal these now in hand go forth vncorrecked to/
except somebody correck them: And what T[indale]. dothe
I wote not/he maketh me nothing of his counsel/I se nothyng
come from him all this longe whyle. wherin with the helpe
that he hathe/that is to saye one bothe to wryte yt and to
correcke it in the presse/he myght haue done it thryse sence
he was first moued to do it. For T[indale]. I know wel was

not able to do yt with out siche an helper which he hathe euer had hitherto.

Aftir this (I saye) consydered / the printer came to me agen and offred me. ij. stuuers and an halfe for the correcking of euery sheet of the copye / which folden contayneth. xvj. leaues/ and for thre stuuers which is. iiij. pense halpeny starling / I promised to do it / so that in al I had for my labour but. xiiij. shylyngis flemesshe [*this amount fixes the number of pages in the tiny volume of this Fourth surreptitious edition, of 2000 copies ; a copy of which is in the Grenville Collection, British Museum. 14 Flemish*=12 *English shillings sterling at 9d. for two sheets of 16 leaves*=32 *sheets or 512 leaves*] which labour / had not the goodnes of the deede and comon profyte and helpe to the readers compelled me more then the money / I wolde not haue done yt for. v. tymes so miche / the copie was so corrupt and especially the table : and yet saith T[indale]. I did it of couetousnes : If this be couetousnes / then was Tindal moche more couetouse / for he (as I her say) toke. x. ponde for his/ correccion. I dyd it also / sayth he / of curiositie and vaynglory / ye and that secretly : and did not put to my name whiche / I saye / be two euydent tokens that I sought no vaynglory / for he that doth a thing secretly and putteth out hys name / how seketh he vaynglory? and yet is not the man ashamed to wryte that vaynglory and couetousnes where my two blynde goides / but I tell Tin[dale]. agen / that if malyce and enuy (for all his holy protestacions) had not bene his two blynde goidis / he wold neuer haue thus falsely / vncharitably / and so spightfully belyed and sclaundred me with so perpetual an infamie. Tin[dale]. saith I walked not aftir the rules of loue and softenes / but let men read how maliciously he belyeth and sclaundereth me for wel doing : and iuge what rule of loue and softnes he obseruethe. It is greate shame to the teacher when his owne deedis and wordis reproue and condempne himself. He hath grete experience of my natural disposicion and complexion saith he. But I wyll not be his Phisicion and decerne his water at this tyme. And as for his two disciplis that gaped so longe for their masters morsel that thei might haue the aduauntage of the sale of his bokis of which one sayd vnto me. It were almose he were hanged that correcketh the testament for the dewch / and the tother harped on his masters vntwned string / saying that because

I englissh Resurreccion the lyfe aftir this / men gatherd that I denied the general resurreccion: which errour (by their own sayng) was gathred longe before this boke was printed / vnto which ether of theis disciples I semed no honest man for correcking the copye / I wil not now name them / nor yet shew how one of them / neuer I dare say seyng. *s. Jerome de optimo genere interpretandi* / yet toke vpon him to teche me how I shuld translat the scripturis / where I shuld geue worde for worde / and when I shulde make scholias / notis / and gloses in the mergent as himself and hys master doith. But in good faithe as for me I had as lief put the trwthe in the text as in the margent and excepte the glose expowne the text (as many of theirs do not) or where the text is playn ynough: I had as lief leue siche fryuole gloses clene out. I wolde the scripture were so puerly and plyanly translated that it neded nether note / glose nor scholia / so that the reder might once swimme without a corke. But this testament was printed or T[indale's]. was begun / and that not by my preuencion [*anticipation*] / but by the printers quicke expedicion and T[indale's]. own longe sleaping / for as for me I had nothing to do with the printing therof / but correcked their copie only / as where I founde a worde falsely printed / I mended it: and when I came to some derke sentencis that no reason coude be gathered of them whether it was by the ignorance of the first translatour or of the prynter / I had the latyne text by me and made yt playn: and where any sentence was vnperfite or clene left oute I restored it agene: and gaue many wordis their pure and natiue significacion in their places which thei had not before. For my conscience so compelled me to do / and not willingly and wetingly to slip ouer siche fautes into the hurte of the text or hinderance of the reder

But to certifye the (good indifferent reder) wyth what conscience and discrecion Tin[dale]. wrote this vnsober pistle agenst me / thou shalt here after se / that of some greuouse crimes he accuseth and condempneth me of an hearsaye or of the informacion by other men.

Tindal *That my curiosite shuld haue drawne no small noumber vtterly to denye the Resurreccion of the bodye / affirming that the soule departed is the spiritual bodie of the resurreccion / and other resurreccion shal there none be.* [*p.* x.]

Joye. This informacion T[indale]. bringeth in / in the

seconde leif of his pistle to confirme the same sclaunderouse lye ymagened of hys owne brayne / adding with a constant affirmacion these wordis.

Tindal *And of al this is George Joyes vnquiet curiosite the hole occasion.* [p. xi.]

Joye. This shameles lye and sclaunderouse affirmacion T[indale]. is not ashamed to prynte / onely because I saye that there is a lyf aftir this wherein the blessed spirits departed lyue in heuen with criste (for this is his wyse argument / he that putteth the soulis in heuen before domes daye stealeth away the resurreccion of their bodyes / Ge. Joye sayth they be in heuen / *ergo* he denyed the resurreccion) but also because he is so enformed. Besydis thys condempnacion of me by hearsaye or enformacion of hys faccyon: he is not ashamed of hys owne brayne to affirme and to wryte it / saying in the same fowrthe peise [*paragraph*] of his pistle thus.

Tindal *Moreouer / ye shal vnderstonde that George Joye hath had of a longe tyme meruelouse ymaginacions about this worde Resurreccion that it shulde be taken for the state of the soulis departed &c.* [p. x.]

Joye. which same meruelouse ymaginacion / John apo. xx. hath: calling that state or lyfe the first resurreccion: Lo. Nowe yf T[indale]. nor yet his wyse enformers cannot proue nor iustifye these sclaunderouse lyes vpon me / as I know well they neuer shall as euery man maye se me in my bokis constantly wrytinge and affirmyng the Resurreccion of our bodyes at domes daye which (I thanke god) I neuer douted of: may ye not se then the maliciouse entent / shrewed purpose / and corrupt conscience of this man for all his holy protestacions / thus temerariously and abominably to write to defame and sclaunder me? Ar not these the venomouse tethe of vepers that thus gnawe a nother mannis name? ar thei not spearis and dartis and their tongues as sharpe as Psal. 57. swerdis as the prophet paynteth them? whette thei Psal. 140. not their tongues lyke serpents? nourysshe thei not adders venome with their lippes? yisse verely. For the psal. 5 trowth is not in their mouthes sayth Dauid :•They are corrupted within / their throte is an open stynkyng graue / wyth their tongues they flater and deceyue. Here may ye smel out of what stynkyng breste and poysoned virulent throte thys peivisshe Pystle spyrethe and breathed forthe.

vnto Tindals pistle.

But yet here first of all / T[indale]. (as ye maye se) accuseth and dampneth me / of coniecture and temerariouse iugement / to be vnhonest / not walking aftir christis rules of loue and softnes / but rather to be a sediciouse persone mouing stryfe and debate / to be vayngloriouse / curiouse / and couetouse and I cannot tell you what. But ere T[indale]. had thus by open writing and prynting it to / accused and dampned me / yt had become him (yf he had wylled to be taken for a cristen man) firste to haue knowne these vices pryuately correcked betwene me and them whom I had with these synnes offended and eft aftir for my incorrigible and vntractable hardnes not hearing the chirche / to haue also offended yt openly casting me out of yt / as crist techeth vs: and not thus fyercely and sodenly of a lyght and false coniecture and temerariouse iugement (I wil say no worse) to preuent [*anticipate*] bothe the iugement of god and man and to vsurpe the offyce of god before he come to iuge vs bothe / nothyng feryng his terrible thretening / saing Juge noman lest ye be iuged / condempne not lest ye be condempned your selues. T[indale]. condemneth mat. 7. Luc. 6. me of curiosite / but iuge (indifferent reder) whither this be not an vnquiet vayn curyouse touche to crepe into a nother mannis conscience curiously to serche accuse and condempne / when he shuld haue descended rather into his own / examining himselfe of what affeccion and minde he wolde write so many lyes and sclaunders of his brother of so light coniecture and heresayes. If I had bene gilty [of] al these fautes / it had bene Tin[dale's]. parte to haue had compassion rather vpon me / to warne / to exhorte me / then so sodenly and spyghtfully to haue had accused me so openly / and that wyth so perpetual and haynouse a sclaunder of my name that himselfe (though he wolde) yet can he not reuoke it and restore it me agene. He shuld haue consydered that god commaundeth vs to be eche others seruants / and not so cruell iuges and condempners / namely of siche light coniectures. what Ro. 14 hath T[indale]. to do to iuge a nother mannis seruant? what folehardines is it to crepe out of our own consciences curiously to serche other mennis hertis? ye and that to iuge and condempne them by open and perpetuall bokis? I haue god my iuge / and therefore nede I not Tindals temerariouse iugement: ether I stande or fall vnto my nown lorde / yea he is redye / yf I fall / merciably to lifte me vp agayn / and to sustayn me that I fall not.

But T[indale]. and his goodly enformers thought / it was no honest mannis touche to correcke a false copye of the testament / which yf yt had not be done at that tyme / ther had bene printed and solde two. M. mo falser bokis then euer before : thys semed no honest touche to them that had bought Tindals copy corrected for ten ponde as I herde saye / and shuld haue the auauntage of the first sale / for it semed to them / that the mo trwer testaments / the lesse to be their auauntage : but had these that I correcked / gone forth falser then eny wother before / and had I refused the correccion of them / and so all the byers and reders to haue ben vtterly deceyued with them / then had I plaid the honest man : then wold not one of them (as he did) haue wisshed me hanged for my labour. But nowe to haue correct that false copy that the testaments myght be the trwlyer prynted for the edifying of the reders / is aftyr T[indale's]. charite / a dede of stryfe and debate / and of one that walketh not aftir the rules of loue and softnes whych Tindale / Christe I shulde saye / and hys disciples teach vs. To correck the false copye that the holy testament myght be the perfytlyer red and vnderstonden / that the reders be not taried nor seduced is now aftir T[indale]. and his enformers a touche of vaynglory / curiosite / and couetousnes blynde gydis &c. For yf I had chaunged neuer a worde in the boke / but onely correcked those wordis whyche were falsely printed before in the copye / yet had T[indale]. in this first peise of his pistle thus accused iuged and condempned me gilty of al these sayd vices as hys own wordis testifye and as euery man maye perceyue his mynde that wil expende and consydere his processe : ioyninge this peise vnto that at foloweth.

Tindal *But when the pryntynge of myne was almost fynesshed / one brought me a copie and shewed me so manye places / in soche wyse altered that I was astonyed and wondered not a lytle what furye had dryuen him to make soche chaunge and to call yt a diligent correction. For thorow oute Mat. Mark and Luke perpetually : and ofte in the actees / and sometyme in John and also in the hebrues / where he fyndeth this worde Resurreccion / he chaungeth yt into the lyfe after this lyfe / or verie lyfe / and soche lyk / as one that abhorred the name of the resurreccion.* [*pp.* ix-x.]

Joye. Se how this man exaggereth and heapeth togyther so many placis so altered making himself to be astonned and to woundre of what furye I was caryed to geue this one worde Resurreccion hys very ryght significacion : and yet of so many places he can shew but one sely worde altered into his right significacion as I haue sufficiently proued / whiche worde in all the thre euangelists telling al the same thing / haue but one and euer the same significacion in those thre placis and in John the. v. cap. and in the hebrewes ca. xj. also a lyke. But and yf Tin[dale]. dirst haue shewed of so many places any one mo so chaunged / men shuld haue plainly sene / my diligent correccion to haue mended his negligent (I wil not saye his false) translacion. And yet he woundreth of what furie I was drouen thus to do. Softe and pacient / good wordis Tindale : and no furiouse fumes / remember your rules of loue and softenes aftir the which a litel before your self pretende to walke / and me to haue broken them / and take not your selfe no more by the nose / prease not so furiously vpon me as to saye I abhorre the name of the Resurreccion for geuing it in his place his right significacion / which I did of no furie but of good zele vnto the trueth / lest the reader myght be seduced with you be-leuing there is no lyfe of soulis departed : but to lye a sleape without heuen tyl domes daye / For in so englysshing the worde I do no more abhorre the name of the resurreccion then do your selfe in the. xj. cap. to the hebrews where youre selfe call yt lyfe also : and haue graunted it me that yt so signifyeth. If I denye the resurreccion for so englysshing yt / so do you denye hell for englisshing *Infernus* a graue.

Tindal *If that chaunce / to turne resurreccion into lyfe after this lyfe / be a dyligent correccion / then must my translacion be fautie in those places / and saynt Jeromes / and all the translatours that euer I heard of in what tonge so euer it be / from the apostles vnto this hys dyligent correccion (as he calleth it) which whither it be so or no / I permit it to other mennes iudgementes.* [*p.* x.]

Joye. whether my correccion in this place be a diligent correccion / and Tin[dale's]. translacion fautye or no / let better lerned then we bothe be iuges. Nether foloweth yt / that for be cause ether myne be diligent / or T[indale]. be fautye / saynt Jerom[e]s (whyche neuer that I red translated it into englisshe) shulde be fautye in latyne / for he translated but oute of greke into latyn (yf he dyd translate it) vnderstanding (I dare saye) by thys worde *Resurrectio* in those places the

lyfe of soulis departed or the first resurreccion as John
apo. 20   calleth yt / and not the generall resurreccion as
Tin[dale] dremeth. S. Jerome knewe ful wel that the worde
in hebrew had mo significacions then the resurreccion of the
flesshe / and did not euery where translate the hebrew verbe
into *Surgo* / as I haue shewed before alleged in Isaye.

Tindal *But of thys I chalenge George Joye / that he did not put his owne name therto and call yt rather his owne tra[n]slacion : and that he playeth boo pepe / and in some of hys bookes putteth in his name and title / and in some kepeth it oute.* [p. x.]

Joye. If George Joye playth bo peep for not putting to his name / then doth Tin[dale]. play bo peep with the testament first translated wher he did not put to his name to avoyd vaynglory: And. S. Paule (by this wyse reason) playd bo peep wythe hys pistle to the hebrews. Also here T[indale]. chalengeth me be cause I called yt not rather my nowne translacion / oh good lorde what occasions this man honteth for agenst me ? Truth yt is that Solomon sayth prouer. xviij. he that delighteth in dissension / taketh of euery thing an occasyon to chyde. Shuld I haue called yt my translacion for correcking the fawty and corrupt copye / or for englisshing resurreccion the very lyfe aftir this ? If I had so done verely T[indale]. had had a iuste cause to haue writen agenst me for lying and stealing awaye the glorie of his name for first translating the testament / But it was happie that the printer in making the title called yt a diligent correccion and not a translacion   T[indale]. here addeth to my name / my title to. I cannot tell what he meaneth by my title : except yt be / that in some of my bokis I write that I was some tyme fellow of Peter College in Camebridge for the more difference betwene a nother man that perchaunce might haue the same name that I haue / And yf thys be the tytle that offendeth T[indale]. I will hence forthe leaue yt oute.

Tindal *It is lawfull for who will / to translate and shew his mynde / though a thousand had translated before him.* [p. x.]

[**Joye.**] why then is T[indale]. thus angrie with me for shewing my mynde (no not my minde but the mynde of crist) vpon thys worde *resurrectio ?*

Tindal *But yt is not lawfull (thynketh me) ner yet expedient for the edifienge of the vnitie of the fayth of christ / that whosoeuer wil / shal by hys awne auctoryte / take another mannes translacion* and put oute and in and chaunge at pleasure / and cal it a correccion. [*p.* x.]

Joye. God forbyd that T[indale]. shulde so thinke of hymselfe / that he hathe so exquysitly / (ye and that at firste) translated the testament that yt cannot be mended / for he aknowlegeth and proueth the contrary himself / and desyerth other men to mende yt : wherefore verely me thought it bothe lawfull and expedyent so to do : ye and that by as good autorite as he did first translate it vnperfaytly. Is yt not lawful to correck that at is amysse lest the readers be ether taryed or seduced ? Aftir orygine / Jerome translated and ofte correcked the psalter and was desyered of Damasus then bishop of Rome to correck the the new testamet / which (I am suer) thought it lawfull and expedient to / as we se dayly / other lerned men other wyse redyng and translating the scriptures then dyd Jerome. Dyd all the olde doctours translate / allege / and rede the scriptures a lyke ? Did they stonde so highly in their own consaight that any one dysdayned to be correcked of a nother ? And shall we then permytte vnto onely Tind[ale]. but a man / farre inferior vnto them both in lerning / iugement / and vertew / to translate and wryte what he lysteth noman so hardy to amende his fautis? what profit and goodnes cometh of the diuersite of translacions / rede S. Austen in his seconde boke *de doctrina christiana* cap. xij. In the chirch of god as there be many and dyuerse membres / so haue they many and sondry giftes / and one may se in a nother mannis workis that he saw not himselfe. And I doute not but there be / and shal come aftir vs / that canne and shall correcke our workes and translacions in many places and make them miche more perfayt and better for the reader to vnderstande / and shulde we therfore brawll and wryte agenst them as T[indale]. dothe agenst me ? god forbyde / but rather thanke them and geue place as Paule teacheth. j. Corinth .xiiij.

Tindal *Moreouer / ye shall vnderstonde that George Joye hath had of a longe tyme maruelouse ymaginacions aboute this worde resurreccion / that it shuld be taken for the state of the soules aftir their departinge from their bodyes / and hath also (though he hath been reasoned with therof and desyred to cease) yet sowen his doctrine by secret letters on that syde the see* [i.e., in England] */ and caused great division amonge the brethren. Insomoch that John Fryth* *beyng in prison in the toure of London / a litle before his death [on 4th July, 1533] / wrote that we shuld warne hym and desyer him to cease / and wolde haue then wryten agaynst him / had I not withstonde him. et cetera.* [*p. x.*]

Joye. If Tindals parte had bene so trwe / and myne so false for translatyng thys worde *Resurrectio* / as he pretendeth: ❡ Tindale falleth from his cause, to lying and sclaundering. he wold haue boden better by it / and haue stoken nerer the probacion therof in his pystle as by the kaye of his whole cause prouing his translacion trwe and myne false : and neuer haue had so farre swaruen from his principal / as (al probacions for his parte / and the confutacions of myn clene forgoten) a man caryed of what furiouse affectis his tragical pistle declareth to fal to belying / defaming and sclaundering of any man : he shuld haue erst proued his parte trw and myn false or he had thus raged and rayled vpon me. But these crimes which he here openly and falsely impingeth vnto me of his own head and cannot iustifye them / he hath promysed before recorde to reuoke. And if he be a trwe crysten man / sithe he cannot iustifye his writing so vncircumspectly put forth and thrusted into many handis / he must ether for fere of that terrible sentence of god thretening al euill spekers / detractours and defamers his vengeaunce and wrath / orels if charite be so farre quenched in his breste as hys maliciouse pistle proueth it / yet at leste wise for very shame of these. iiij. honest men / before whom and eft sens before me he promised to reuoke his writing of me / he muste now reuoke his sclaunderouse and lying pistle wherin he sayth that I abhorre the name of the resurreccion and that I shuld denie it. Also here he imputeth vnto me certain crimes of which he condempneth me of heresaye / ye and that by the enformacion of other / That no small noumber thorow my curiosite vtterly denye the resurreccion of the bodyes &c. lo / good reader / Thus is not T[indale]. ashamed nor afraid to write at th[e]enformacions (if there be eny sich) of other men. T[indale]. shuld haue first considred what men these were that so falsely enformed him / and of what stomak and proof thei enformed him. For this dare I say constantly (I haue yet the copie of the letters writen but onely vnto one man / in which as euery man may se / it may be assone and as lykely gathered that I denye that there is any god as the resurreccion / but I do rather affirme yt / or that onely the soule departed is the spiritual bodie of the resurreccion as T[indale]. is enformed and here affirmeth the same to confirme thys false enformacion. T[indale]. and his enformers shuld haue turned fyrst to the article in our *credo* concerning the resurreccion which I translated / loking whether I do not affirme it / and like wise in all placis of scripture where so euer I fynde this worde *Resurrectio* signifying the resurrection of oure bodyes.) But I dare saye: that yf Tindals enformers whom by name I coude drawe out into light (if T[indale]. saye it not of his owne head) were examined of this reporte / that as they cannot for shame affirme and shew it to be taken of my letters / so shulde T[indale]. with miche more shame to haue bene afrayd openly to wryte it / adding this adsercion of his owne brayne.

Tindal *And of all this is G. Joyes vnquyet curiosite the hole occasion / whether he be of the sayde faccion also / or not / to that let him answer him selfe.* [*p*. xi.]

Joye. Al this forsayd peise therfore is nothinge els (I take god to recorde) but a continuall shamelesse lye and a perpetual spightful sclaunder maliciously blowne togyther vpon me out of Tin[dale's]. mouthe. These false lyes and enuyouse infamyes whether they can come forth of any cristen breste or stande with siche holy adiuracions and protestacions as he paynteth aftirward to colour his ypocrysy and deadly hatered so long conceyued / noureshed in his brest and now spitted oute vpon me let euery man iuge /

For as for me / god know[e]th / I neuer had other ymaginacion aboute this worde resurreccion then the significacion whych I haue sufficiently declared. And if euer I had any wother ymaginacions then that whiche in some placis (as I haue translated it) it signifyeth / euen the ferme faste permanent lyfe of the soulis departed: and agene in some placis the resurreccion of the flesshe as I haue declared yt / I adpele / prouoke / and compell Tindals conscience to tell yt openly / and yf he cannot / let him confesse his lye and knowleg how shamelessly he sclaundereth me and reuoke it. Also where he sayth / that I haue ben reasoned wyth all and desyered to ceasse: it is true that I reasoned with him of this mater twise or or thryse and tolde him that he did well yf he reuoked his erroneouse doctryne sowne so ofte in hys bokis: and if he saith that it was he that desyered me to ceasse / I reasoned wyth none els but onely with him / in good faith I shal tel the trwthe / we neuer reasoned the mater but thorow his impacience our disputacion euer ended with chyding and brawling in somiche that aftirwarde in hys exposicion vpon John he stretched forth his penne agenst me as farre as he dirst / but yet spared my name / at the whiche chaleng I winked / yet taking yt not as ment of me because I loued quyetnes not wylling that any man shuld know what hatred he did euer beare me sence I came ouer /

For when he coude not avoyd the manyfest scriptures nor soyle the reasons brought agenst him / then the man began to fume and chaafe calling me fole / vnlerned / with other obprobriouse names: then I knew not the scriptures nor what I sayd &c. and except T[indale]. call this his charitable desyer and louing monicion wherwith he desyerd me to ceasse / in good fayth I neuer herd whother of hys mouthe. I am sory to wryte this / but hys deadly lyes and maliciously sclaunders compel me to do yt.

Tindal Then sayth he that I haue *sowne my doctryne by secrete letters on that syde the sea* [*i.e.*, in England] *and caused grete diuision emonge the bretherne &c.* [*p. x.*]

Joye. I neuer wrote letter concerning this mater I take god to recorde but vnto one man seduced by his false doctryne / whych yet (I thynke) persysteth for all my letters in the same opinion / so wholly dependeth he vpon Tindals mouth addicte vnto hys wordis / that the soulis sleap oute of heuen tyll domes daye / whom I warned at last to ceasse wryting any more of this mater to me / and not to stande ouer miche in hys own consayght nor yet to depende ouer myche of any mannis doctryne / declaring him fyrst the significacions of this worde *resurrectio* as I haue done in thys Apologye /

And yet haue I here the copye of my letters sent vnto this man whych I neuer desyered as euery man shall se to be kept secrete / nether dyd the yonge man so kepe them for they and their copyes went thorow many handis as I vnderstode aftir / and were sent vnto Frithe in the tower / wherof Frith wrote thys warnyng to Tin[dale] whyche he here mencyoneth /

and I answerd Frith agene by my letters / but aftir I answered him / I neuer herde more from Frith of this mater / and yet had he a longe tyme aftir in the tower to haue wryten / if he had sene his parte good:

Frith wrote tindals answers to More for tindale / and corrected them in the prynte / and printed them to at Amelsterdam / and whether he winked at T[indale's]. opinion as one hauyng experience of Tindals complexion / or was of the same opinion I cannot tel / the man was ientle and quyet and wel lerned and better shuld haue ben yf he had liued. Then sayth T[indale].

Tindal *Thereto I haue ben sence enformed that no small nowmber thorow hys curiosite denie the resurrecion of the flessh and bodie.* [*p.* xiv.]

Joye. Thou seist (good reader) how that I denie not the general resurreccion / nor I my self neuer thought it to be denyed but haue constantly affirmed and taught it. But thou remembrest euerywhere T[indale's]. argument / thus argwing full falsely: If the soulis be in heuen /*ergo* there shalbe no resurreccion of their bodyes. Here tindals faccion and his disciples argew and beleue lyke their Master / sayng: lo George Joye sayth the soulis be in heuen / wherfore it muste nedis folow that he denyeth the resurreccion of their bodyes / or els he muste make oure Master and father tindale a lyer and his doctrine false / here may euery man se how T[indale]. playth bo peepe wyth me impynging heresy vnto me / for confuting hys errour sowne hitherto in his bokis:

Tindal yet sayth T[indale] to / that these men seduced by my doctryne affirme *that the soule / when she is departed / is the spiritual bodye of the resurreccion: and other resurreccion shall there non[e] be.* [*p.* xiv.]

Joye. If T[indale]. can shew me these wordes to be mine ether in writing / or brynge forthe any man that euer herde me speke them / then let me suffer dethe. For I take god to recorde that I neuer thought them / and sence I red my philosophy / I knew the difference betwene a bodye and the soule / and was neuer so mad as to call the soule a spirituall bodye / as Tyndal sayth I do affirme yt: but T[indale]. in deed when I argewed that sleape in scrypture was onely appropryated vnto the bodie and not to the soule / and a shuttyng vp of the sencis frome their vse / he graunted me that the soule of man was also a bodely substaunce: wherat a non I perceyued his highe lerning.

Tindal At last saith T[indale]. *I haue talked wyth some of them my selfe so dotyd in thai foyle that it were as good to perswade a poste as to plucke that madnes oute of their* braynes. *And of this all is George Joyes vnquiet curiosite the hole occasion.* [*pp* x.-xi.]

Joye. If any man list to beleue T[indale] / that he hath thus talked wyth some so doted / lete him so do in gods mane [*name*]. For as for me / sithe I se him lye so manifestly in other thingis / suerly I trust him the lesse in thys tale: nor wil I neuer beleue him til he bringeth forthe some one so doted / For I thinke there be none so mad / And whether I be so curiouse and vnquiet as he reporteth me / lete them be iuges that se my workis and rede this mine answere and know my conuersacion. And here T[indale]. addeth this tayle to knyt vp his lies sayng /

Tindal *whether he be of the sayd faccion also or not / to that let him answer himselfe.* [*p.* xi.]

Joye. I am not affraid to answere Master Tindal in thys mater for all his high lernyng in hys hebrewe greke latyne &c. T[indale]. supposeth / ye he affirmeth yt here twise for fayling / that I am of the same faccion And I answere and tel T[indale]. agene that he belyeth me deadly / and that nether he nor noman els can gather one iote of al the wryting and wordes that euer I spake or wrote / that I shulde once thynke that there shuldbe no general resurreccion of our bodyes / nor yet that the soules departed shulde onely be the spiritual bodyes of the resurreccion. Blame me not (I beseche the cristen reader) though I seme in this place vnpacient: For verely I am spightfully prouoked and exasperated with his lyes and sclaunders thus penned into my perpetuall infamy / and am compelled to defende my name and fame which ther is nothing to me more dere and leife / for there is no kynde of infamy so pernicius as is to be sclaundered of heresye / whych Tin[dale]. impingeth vnto me / nothing consydering that (though he wolde) yet can he not restore me my name agene / And I meruel that this so holy a man as he pretendeth himselfe forgetteth what paule threteneth sayng that i. cor. vj these euyll spekers bye / and sclaunderers shalnot possede the heretage and kingdome of god / I pray god geue this man a better mynde and to printe wel in his hert and remember his own doctrine / and to feare hys own terrible othe and so harde and perellouse desyer in thys hys pistle: thus saying here aftir.

Tindal *More ouer I take god (whych alone seith the hert)* to recorde to my conscience / beseching him that my parte be not in the bloude of crist / yf I wrote of all that I haue written thorow out all my boke / aught of an euil purpose / of enuy or malice to eny man &c.   [p. xii.]

Tindal *If George Joye wil saye (as I wot well he will) that his chaunge is the the scene. &c.*   [p. xi.]

Joye George Joye hath sayd yt and proued yt to / that yt is the meanyng of the scryptures in that place / And T[indale]. had ben so pacient as he pretendeth when euery man saye as he sayth / and loke vp and woundre at his wordis: he wolde haue taryed other mennis iugement / and not haue thus maliciously auenged hym selfe preuenting yt wyth so poysoned a pistle.

[**Tindal.**] *But though yt were the verie meanynge &c.*

[**Joye.**] Lo here may ye se how highly thys man standeth in his owne opinion / thynking that his false translacion ought not to geue place to the trwe meanyng of the scryptures put in of a nother man: nether do I here at my nowne pleasure put in my meanyng but the meaning of crist as hymself expowneth it / whose meaning is not the next waye to stablysshe heresyes as Tindals meaning dothe / as I haue playnely proued / which let me se yf he can improue and confute: but rather to confute T[indale's]. heresye which is that the soulis sleap out of heuen feling nether payne nor ioye til domes daye.

Tindal *As for an ensample / when Christ sayth Jo. v. The tyme shall come in the which all that are in the graues shall heare his voyce and shall come me forth: they that haue done good vnto resurreccion of lyfe / or with the resurreccion of lyfe / and they haue done euel / vnto the resurreccion or with the resurreccion of damnacion. George Joyes correccion is / they that haue done good shall come forth into the verie lyfe / and they that haue done euell into the lyfe of damnacion / thrustinge cleane oute this worde resurreccion.*   [p. xi.]

Joye He that geueth this worde resurreccion his very trw significacion in his place thrusteth not out the worde / but declareth yt playnly and putteth it in / as he that translateth thys worde *Deus* / calling yt god in englysshe / thrusteth not out god / but putteth him for them to know him in englisshe which vnderstande not the latyn. If Tin[dale]. translate theis wordis / *paradisum voluptatis* / calling them a garden in

Eden / and a nother come aftir him englisshyng the same a pleasaunt paradise / this man thrusteth not clene out paradise. Nether where he translateth And Jacob blessed Pharao / and a nother translateth the same sayng / And Jacob thanked Pharao / yt folowthe not that therfore this man thrusteth out clene this worde *Benedixit* / no more then he thrusteth out Paulis soule / that translateth this place of paule. we desyerd not onely to geue vnto you the gospel of god but also our owne lyues or our owne selues / for which Tin[dale]. sayth our own soulis.

Gen. xlvij

Thes. ij.

Tindal *Now by the same auctorite / and with as good reason shall another come and saye of the rest of the text / they that are in the sepulchres / shall heare his voyce / that the sence is / the soules of them that are in the sepulchres shall heare his voyce / and so put in his dyligent correccion and mocke oute the text / that it shal not make for the resurreccion of the flesshe / which thynge also George Joyes correccion doth manifestlye affirme.* [p. xi.]

Joye. I wolde know of Tinda[le]. whether when a mannis bodye is dead and layd in graue / yt be his dead bodye or hys soule that hereth cristis voyce / I am suer T[indale]. is not so farre besydis his comon sencis as to saye the dead bodye hereth cristis voyce / *ergo* yt is the soule that hereth yt / and then why dothe T[indale]. despyse my sence or rather the trw sence of the scripture calling it a mocking out of the text and a false glose? I am suer Tin[dale]. will not vnderstand the textis of Peter / that the gospell is preched to the dead bodyes in graue but rather to the soulis departed / Albeit I se in hys new correccion how shamefully and of what corrupt mynde god knowth / he hathe peruerted thys text / wyth thys note / That the dead ar the ignorant of god. when there the dead and quyke be taken as they stonde in the *credo* / the deade euen for the departed out of this worlde and the quyk for them that lyue there in: whych article that criste shal iuge them bothe / as it is setforth for the playn peple so is it playnly spoken as the letter sowneth / and not in a mistik allegory worthy any sich a false glose in the mergent / T[indale]. shuld haue loked beter on the circumstance of the texte / and not haue englisshed / *vt iudicarentur quidem secundum homines carne*: that thei shuld be condempned of men in the flesshe. For by thys peruertyng of the text men may se that T[indale]. hath forgotten his grammer / or els god

i. Pet. 3 and. 4

i. pe. 4

know[e]th of what mynde he wold haue here / *mortuis* / not to signifye the departed oute of this worlde / and *iudicarentur* to signifye that they shuld be condempned / and *secundum homines* / of men. whiche sentence he translated at first truely / and now corrected it *de meliore in peius*: as euery lerned / ye and vnlerned may se / T[indale]. sayth I take away the texte from him in this one worde *resurrectio*: but he in this place / I dare saye / and can proue it to his face / that he corrupteth the text / and by his false translating it / taketh awaye the trwe vnderstonding therof from as many as rede yt / and beleue his translacion.

Nether dothe he that saythe the soulis of the dead shal here cristis voyce / denye the resurreccion of the flesshe: for they maye / and do bothe stande well togither. Criste had al power geuen him in heuen and erthe aftir his dethe and resurreccion / and that euen the power to preserue the dead alyue in their soulis which power of god he tolde the Saduceis they knew not / and yet by his godhed he did daily execute yt: he had powr also to iuge / althoughe he be the sonne of man / whiche powr then geuen him is not idle and voyd til domes daye / but is dayly executed in the partic[u]lare iugement of euery soule departed (yf T[indale]. graunteth any parti[u]clare iugement at al but wil saye the soulis sleape) and then is not this the trwe sence of John in this place? that the soulis of the bodyes resting and sleaping in graue shall here cristis voice and come forthe into that very lyfe which they now lyue and crist proued it vnto the Saduces? John (I saye) beyng so plentuouse in telling one thing so ofte and so many ways / sayd the same thing twise be fore / once thus: verely verely I saye vnto you / who so here my worde / and beleue him that sent me / hath lyfe euerlastyng and shalnot come into condempnacion / but is passed ouer from dethe to lyfe / And aftir warde he expressith yt playnely to be verifyed euen of the dead / the tyme of his iugement in his manhed then standing vpon or beyng present / saynge verely verely I say vnto you / The tyme shal Joan 5 come / and euen now yt is: when euen the dead shal here the voice of the sone of god / and who so here yt shal lyue: which powr of the sone / to be receyued of the father / and in that to be egal with him declared / he resumeth the same sentence yet agen the thirde tyme / sayng. Meruel not at this thyng/for the tyme shall come in which al that ar in graues shal here his voyce and they that haue done good shal come forthe into that verye lyfe/and they that haue done yll into that myserable or dampnable lyfe. For where he sayd before/the dead shal here his voice/now he sayth for the same/all that ar in graues shall here his voyce/and where he sayd in the first same sentence/ar passed frome dethe to lyfe and haue euerlasting life/in the seconde sentence he sayth/shal lyue/and in the thirde and last of all he saythe/shal come forth in to that very and perfit lyfe/ and where he sayd before/condempnacion/here at last he calleth the same the lyfe of condempnacion or dampnable lyfe/as yt is the comon phrase of scripture to saye *spiritus sanctificationis/pro spiritu sancto et sanctitas veritatis pro vera sanctitate* with many siche lyke/Also yt is to be noted that there is none of th[e]euangelistis nor apostles so plentuouse in expowning himselfe with so many wordis and so ofte repeting one thing as is John/vsyng thys particle (*Et*) in englyssh as myche to saye as (*And*) expositiue: that is to expowne the

Jo. vi.   sentence or worde before/as when he saythe who so come to me shall not hongre/and whoso beleue in me shall neuer thirst/there thys particle (*and*) expowneth what yt is to come to Crist/that is to saye to beleue in Criste/

Jo. xj.   And when he saythe: I am the resurreccion and lyfe/there thys worde (*and*) expowneth what resurreccion sygnifyeth/euen very lyfe/and so the sentence folowyng

Jo. iij.   declareth yt. And agen where he saith except a man be borne of water and the spirit &c there/this worde (*And*) signifyeth/that is to saye of the spirit/expowning

Esaye. xliiij   what water is in that place as Isay expowneth

Jo. vij.   water/and John also. But and if T[indale]. wil nedis saye styll that I mocke out the Resurreccion of the flesshe/ because I say that the soulis of them that be in graues shal here his voyce/I answer and aske him what mok is ther in these my wordis to saye that aftir the general resurreccion/ the soulis with the bodis that were in graue shall come forthe into that lyfe euerlasting? Is not this a trewe and catholyk sence? can T[indale]. make it false?

But yet here wolde I aske T[indale]. (yf he wolde not iuge me curiouse) a nother question/euen this: whether that the bodies shal ryse be fore thei come forthe of

their graues / and so come forthe into that perpetual lyfe /
or whether theï shal first come forthe of their graues
and then rise aftirwarde? If he saythe they must ryse
before they come forthe vnto that very lyfe / then is yt
trwe that they shall not come forthe vnto the resurreccion /
for they be now rysen al redye and the resurreccion is
past wyth them / and then is my translacion trwe that they
shal come forthe into that very lyfe / and not vnto the resurreccion of their bodyes as T[indale]. saythe. And yf he wyll
saye / to make this worde resurreccion to signifie the resurreccion of the flesshe (lest it be mocked out as he saythe /
whiche noman entendeth) that the bodies firste come forthe
of their graues and then ryse aftirwarde / then is his translacion as trew and as lyke / As the man that lyeth him down to
slepe vpon his bed in his chamber first to come forthe of his
chamber before he ryseth out of his bed / lo (reader) here
thou seist whother Tin[dale]. is brought for so supersticyously
steking to onely one significacion of this worde *Resurrectio.*
Now let T[indale]. beware lest emong so many his friuole notis
and gloses in mergents some of them be fownde bothe false
and sclaunderouse and to litle effect. For as for my englisshing of the worde / is proued manifestly to be the very text.

[**Tindal.**] And at laste where T[indale]. sayth / that in
his mynde *a lytle vnfayned loue aftir the rules of criste &c.* [*p.* xi.]

Joye. I thynke that siche loue may not stande with
cristis rules / orels Tindals loue is miche worthe whiche
hathe fayned vtwardly to haue loued me / when all this while
he did but nouresshe in his breste hatered and malice longe
a go conceyued and now at laste hathe spewed forthe al his
venome and poyson at once vpon me.

Tindal *Wherfore / concernynge the resurreccion / I protest before
god and oure sauioure Jesus Crist / and before the vniuersall congregacion that beleueth in him / that I beleue according to the open
and manyfest scriptures and catholyck fayth / that Christ is rysen
agayne in the flesshe whych he receaued of his mother the blessed
virgin marie and bodye wherin he dyed. And that we shal all
both good and bad ryse both flesshe and bodye / and apere together
before the iugement seat of crist / to receaue euery man accordynge
to his dedes. And that the bodyes of all that beleue and continew
in the true fayth of christ / shalbe endewed with lyke immortalite
and glorye as is the bodye of christ.* [*pp.* xi-xii.]

Joye. Tin[dale]. nedeth not to make so longe an holy protestacion of thys mater/for noman layth yt to hys charge: but let Tin[dale]. clere himselfe of this errour that he hathe wryten thryse in his answere to M. More and in his exposicion of John : That is to weit that he saithe the soulis departed slepe and shall not be in heuen tyll domes daye/and yet affirmeth arrogantly and argeweth vnwysely/that whoso shulde saye the contrary/denyeth the general resurreccion.

Tindal *And I protest before god and oure sauioure christ and al that beleue in him / that I holde of the soules that are departed as moche as maye be proued by manifest and open scripture / and thinke the soules departed in the fayth of christ and loue of the lawe of god / to be in no worse case then the soule of Christ was / from the tyme that he deliuered his spryte into the handes of his father / vntyll the resurreccion of hys bodye in glorye and immortalite. Neuerthelater / I confesse openly / that I am not persuaded that they be all readie in the full glorie that crist is in / or the elect angels of God are in. Nether is yt anye article of my fayth : for yf yt so were / I se not but then the preachynge of the resurreccion of the flesshe were a thinge in vayne. Not withstondinge yet I am readie to beleue it / if it may be proued with open scripture.* [*p.* xii.]

Joye. Now thanked be god/that Tin[dale]. at last hath fownde oute that doctryne whyche crist nor hys apostles neuer taught/nor was not in the worlde at that tyme. God be preased that haue shewed T[indale]. that depe secrete layd vp in hys tresury/Now he thinketh that the soulis departed be in no worse case then was cristis spirit from hys dethe vntyl his resurreccion/but cristis spirit was in heuen : *ergo* T[indale]. stealeth awaye the resurreccion of cristis bodye and our bodyes to/

Tindal But Tin[dale]. thus come home/now shifteth and seketh this sterting hole sayng that if they be in heuen in as ful and perfit glory as crist is in/or the electe aungels (and yet of this full and perfit glory noman contendeth with him) then he seith not els but that *the preching of the resurreccion were in vayne.* [*p.* xii.]

Joye. No forsothe : The resurreccion is so necessary an article of our faythe that in what Joye soeuer the soulis be/ yet we must beleue yt and preche it to/orels make cristis doctryne false and saye that himself is not rysen. And here can I not meruel ynoughe at T[indale's]. ignorance of the

scriptures/whyche declare playnely that the glorye and ioye
of the soulis is more ful and perfit when they shal haue their
bodyes felows and parte takers of their felicite and ioye whom
they had once as ministers of their good workis and par-
takers of their affliccions/then when they haue their glory
a lone wyth out their bodyes. For vnto this fulnes and
gloriouse perfeccion Paule loked with sore sighes to come
when the hole intire bodye of crist and ful nowmbir of his
electe shall come in altogither aftir the resurreccion of their
bodyes/sayng That all creatures longe for the de- rom. 8.
lyuerance oute of their seruitute into that gloriouse libertye
of the childeren of god: and we our selfe longe sore and
abyde for that adopcion euen the redempcion of our luce. 21
bodyes. For then the soulis shal resume their own bodyes
not mortal but immortal/incorruptible/spiritual/ i. cor. 15
and gloriouse for euer. And yf this werre not a more ful and
perfyter state then the glorye that yet is but of the soulis a
lone/yt shulde not be so sore sighed and longed fore of paule
and euery faythefull that thus beleueth of the redemption/
adopcion/and libertie of their bodyes whych yet ether slepe
in the duste or lyue in trouble affliccion / corrupcion / mortalite/
ignomynie &c. Also in the actis/Luke remembreth Act. iij
thys perfeccion and full state callyng yt the tyme of refrigery
and confort of the presence of god and tyme of the restoring
of all thyngis. And Paule expressing this gloriouse He. xi.
perfeccion and perfit glorye of bothe bodyes and soulis togither aftir the general resurreccion/sayth. All these thorow
fayth deseruyng thys testimony haue not yet receyued the
promyse (that is to saye the intire renewing/redempcion/
and resurreccion of their bodies promised them) because that
god had prouided this one beter thyng for vs/that is to wete/
that thei without vs shuld not be made ful and perfite or be
set faste in their ful glorye of bothe body and soule. For
then shal the vniuersal and intire corps of criste his hole
chirche be made ful and perfit in hir most gloriouse and perfit
state and perpetual fruicion ioyned in ioye euerlasting vnto
hir head Jesu criste. But Tin[dale]. sayth he is not persuaded
that they be all redye in the ful glorie that crist is in/as
thoughe this were not playn in the scriptures/that crist is
there bothe body and soule/and so be not yet the electe:
But yet when the electe shal be there with their bodyes/

they shal not haue so full and perfayth glory as criste hathe.

Tindal And I haue desired George Joye to take open textes that seme to make for that purpose / as this is. To daye thou shalt be with me in paradise / to make therof what he coulde / and to let his dreames aboute thys worde resurreccion goo. For I receaue not in the scripture the priuat interpretacion of any mannes brayne / without open testimony of eny scriptures agreinge thereto. *[p. xii.]*

Joye. T[indale]. neuer desyered me except his obprobrious wordis and reuyling of me were his desyere / And in dead I brought the same text agenst him / and he made a glose of paradice and sayd yt was not there taken for heuen / where euery man may se yt taken for heuen: for crist sayd thou shalt be wyth me / whiche was in heuen. Nether is the interpretacion of that worde resurreccion my priuat interpretacion / but cristis owne interpretacion as I haue proued yt.

Tindal Moreouer I take god (which alone seeth the hert) to recorde to my conscience / besechinge him that my parte be not in the bloude of crist / yf I wrote of al that I haue writen thorow out all my boke / ought of an euell purpose / of enuye or malice to anye man / or to stere vp any false doctrine or opinion in the churche of crist &c. *[p. xii.]*

Joye. Here is an holy othe broken / and a perellouse desyer / yf the contrary to be trewe / For here he rayleth vpon me / he belyeth me / he sclaundereth me and that most spightfully with a perpetual infamye: whiche al yf yt be not of enuy / malice / and hatered of what els shulde yt spring? And euen here for all his holy protestacions / yet herd I neuer sobre and wyse man so prayse his owne workis as I herde him praise his exposicion of the v. vj. and. vij. ca. Mat. in so myche that myne eares glowed for shame to here him / and yet was it Luther that made it / T[indale]. onely but translating and powldering yt here and there with his own fantasies. which praise methought yt then better to haue ben herde of a nother mannis mouth / for it declared out of what affeccion yt sprang euen farre vnlyk and contrarye vnto these whiche he now professeth and protesteth so holely for wordis be the messageris of mennis myndis.

Tind[al]. Saue onlye of pitie and compassion I had and yet haue on the blindnes of my brethren / and to bringe them vnto the knowledge of christ / and to make euery one of them / yf yt were possible as perfect as an angeli of heauen. *[pp. xii-xiii.]*

Joye. Lo here may ye se the good purpose and godly entent of thys good man / and yet hath he by thys his vncharitable / sediciouse / sclaunderouse and lying pistle offended and hurt many a good simple man / and caused them to caste their bokis clene awaye neuer to loke on them more / nor to beleue vs what so euer we haue or shall wryte / thus hath he destroyd that whyche god hathe thorow vs hitherto bylded / and caused vs bothe / ye and the gospel to / to be euill spoken of: besyds the grete reioyse and gaudye mynystred to the enymes of the trowth / ye and some good men wysshe vs bothe neuer to haue ben borne / and saye we be bothe full of poyson. For doutelis Tindals complexion is siche / that for all his holy protestacions and holyer fayned good entents here expressed of his owne mouthe / yet had he leuer marre and destroy al / and (as they saye) set all at six and seuen / then he wolde haue suffred the translacion of this one worde resurrection to haue taryed and aboden the iugement of cristis chirche: so sore yt gnaweth his herte to be correcked and warned of me / but a fole and vnlerned as he bothe reputeth me and telleth yt me to my face /

For in good fayth / and as I shal answere before god / ere he came to one place of the testament to be last corrected / I tolde his scrybe / euen him that wrote and correckted the testament for him / that there was a place in the begynnyng of the. vj. cap. of the actis somwhat derkely translated at fyrst / and that I had mended it in my correction and bode him shew yt Tin[dale]. to mende yt also / yf yt be so sene vnto him / and I dare saye he shewd yt him / but yet because I fownde the fawte and had corrected yt before / Tin[dale]. had leuer to haue let yt (as he did for all my warnyng) stande styll derkely in his new correccion whereof the reder myght take a wrong sence / then to haue mended yt whyche place whether yt standeth now clerer and trwer in my correccion then in his / let the lerned iuge. The place is this / In those dayes as the nowmber &c. where / for that at he translateth wydows: I saye / their pore nedye / which includeth bothe men and wemen / for bothe were releifed by their dayly almose and the greke worde is the comon gender to bothe / and where Tin[dale]. sayth / dayly minystracion / I saye dayly almose as Paule vseth the same worde. ij. corin. ix. For aftir Tindalis translacion / yt sowneth that the apostles shulde haue had certayn wedews of the hebrewes to serue and mynyster vnto them at their tables or in other vses / and so the grudge to haue rysen / that theise wydews were despysed and put out of offyce / when the text trwly and clerely translated sheweth a nother sence farre vnlyke yt as the circumstance declareth. And yf I had ben giltye al these crymes which T[indale]. falsely imputeth vnto me calling me vayngloriouse / couetouse / curiouse / sedyciouse / factiouse a sower of heresyes / a denyer of the general resurreccion whych I take god to recorde I neuer thought nor did yt / he wolde rather (yf he had had siche a godly zele as he here cloketh) ere he had thus openly and perpetually belyed and sclaundered me / fyrst haue come to me and warned me brotherly and paciently / But god almyghty th[e]enseer and sercher of herte and reynes how holy so euer owr vysard wordis and workis apere / be iuge at our departing betwene T[indale]. and me.

I shewed and now I shew T[indale]. agene where the scripture disalow[s] his false opinion of the soulis to slepe / and ye se how he beareth yt /

I shewd T[indale]. where I fownde fawtis longe before this in his translacion and now ye se that he do not onely not mende yt nor confesse not his ignorance but rather call me heretyke and belye me thus spightfully for my labour.

Tindal *wherfore I beseche George Joye / ye and all other to / for to translate the scripture for them selues / whether oute of Greke / Latyn / or Hebrue.* [*j*. xiii.]

Joye. Here T[indale]. is afrayd lest any man wolde steale awaye frome him the glorye and name of his translacion: whych nether I / nor no man els is aboute to do / he wolde haue men translate for them selfe / when we be all borne to profite our neybours and for the comon wele / by his foxisshe ensample he pretendeth as thoughe I shulde steale awaye his gloriouse name for the translacion / and yet he seith and repeteth my wordis himself calling yt but a dyligent correccion and no translacion / for yt had ben but a lye to cal yt my translacion for translatyng and mending a fewe certayn doutful and derke places. But I doubt not / but that aftir T[indale]. and me bothe / there be or shal come / which shall mende bothe our translacions and paraduenture cal them theirs / which I pray god sende vs / and I / for my parte shal geue place vnto siche one withe grete and many thankis.

Tindal *For this I protest / that I prouoke not Joye ner any other man (but am prouoked / and that after the spytfullest maner of prouokinge) to do sore agaynst my wil and with sorow of harte that I now do.* [*pp.* xiii–xiv.]

Joye. If this be not a spightful prouokacion to me / thus to belye me / to sclaunder me as Tin[dale]. hath done / let all that rede bothe our talis be iuge / and whether the englisshing of that worde *resurrectio* be so spightful a prouocacion to a meke modest cristen man / as thus so spightfully and sclaunderously to wryte agenst me.

Tindal T[indale]. sayth *I neuer can nor wil suffer of any man that he shall go take my translacion and correcke yt with out name.* [*p.* xiv.]

Joye. Lo here is a grete mater wherfore this so pacient a man shulde be offended and moued thus shamelesly to wryte into the offense and hurte / ye into the destruccion of al that is buylded in cristis chirche / and perpetual infamy of his brother / let euery man be ware how he medle withe T[indale]. workis / and especially take hede that he mende not / nor yet correck them / except he putto his name / For how false so euer they be / Tin[dale]. wilnot gladly haue them mended as I perceyue / thinkyng that no man is able to correcke hym / and yet vnder the cloke of hipocrysye himselfe desyereth in the ende of his fyrste translacion other men to mende and correcke yt / thys man belyke when he translated yt / was nether man nor angell but god himselfe that cannot erre nor lye /

Tindal he saythe *I haue made siche changing as hym selfe dirst not do as he hopeth to haue hys parte in criste thoughe the hole worlde should be geuen hym for his labour.* [*p.* xiv.]

Joye. And I saye / I haue made many changes which yf T[indale]. had had siche sight in the greke as he pretendeth and conferred yt diligently with the greke as he sayth he did / he shulde haue made the same changes him selfe / which places I shal poynt him to here after / but yet let Tindale loke ouer his Testament once agene and conferre yt a lytle beter withe the verite and greke to / I wolde euery man wolde compare my correccion wyth his / and marke well euery change / and he shall se that I changed some wordis and sentencis / which T[indale]. aftir me was compelled euen as I did / so to change and correcke them himselfe.

Aftir that Tindals correccion was printed: yt chaunced me to turne here and there in his new diligently corrected testament so compared wyth the greke: as first in the beginning of. j. ca. Ro. And there me thought his translacion was not accordyng to the text / where Paule in hys salutacion apereth to affirme that by thre thyngis especially / as the scrypture shewth yt / Criste was declared to be the sonne of god. First by power / secondarely by the holy gost / thirdely in that he rose from dethe. where the text hath / *ex eo quod resurrexit* &c. which T[indale]. englissheth sence the tyme that he rose / knowing not what / *Ex eo* / there sygnifyeth / For criste was declared to be the sonne of god bothe by hys godly powr and also by the holy goste often tymes before his resurreccio and not after yt / as ye maye se hys power in doing miracles all before his resurreccion / the holigost also before yt declaring hym / John. j. xv. and. xvj. Also in the. xiiij. ca. j. cor. how englissheth he there this worde / *spiritus*? which signifyeth in that place the breathe / and voice of our tongue / and yet T[indale]. sayth. If I pray with tongues my spirit prayth / but my mynde is with oute frute / whych sentence aftir hys translacion is contrary to cristis sayng that wolde haue vs to praye and worship his father in spirit. Joan. iiij. ro. j. In that chap. also what englissh geueth Tin[dale]. these wordes *propheta* and prophecie? which signifie there / the interpretour and interpretacion or prechyng of holy scriptures. And where Paule wolde that these interpretours or prechers shuld preche and declare the scriptures one aftir a nother before the congregacion / and not two or thre of them all at once to avoyde confusion / For god (sayth he) is not the autor of confusion &c. T[indale]. euen clene contrary to the text / translateth thus: let the prophetis speke two at once or thre at once. There were some heretyks in paulis tyme which sayd that our bodyes shulde not ryse the selfe same
I. co. 15   ageyn / but wother distincte and seuerall bodies: vnto whose opinion (al be it I know wel T[indale]. beleueth yt not) yet he ministreth a shrewd occasion in taking awaye the texte by vntrwly translating this sentence. *et vnicuique seminum dat deus suum* or *proprium corpus* / (as hathe the vulgare texte) God geueth to euery sead his own bodye / and not a seuerall bodye as T[indale]. translateth yt / For by this text Paule confuteth their heresye / that saye we shal not

ryse agene wyth our own bodyes/but with some wother
seueral and distincte bodyes from these which we now carye
aboute. I meruel that T[indale]. calleth *suum* or *proprium
corpus*/a seueral bodye/If I had thus translated these places
he might wel haue sayd/I had nede go lerne my donate and
accidence agene/rather then to translate scriptures: had he
not yet haue sayd worse by me. But here peraduenture
Tin[dale]. will excuse him by the greke or by some hebrew
phrase left theryn/as he telleth some simple reders that
know nether of them bothe how they make agenst me in thys
worde *resurrectio*: and as he bosteth himselfe in the beginning
of this his godly pistle and also in his prologe/

Tindal saying that he hath compared the testament with
the greke and weded out of yt many fautis (*and yet in some
place made yt worse then it was before*) which lake of helpe at
the beginnyng and ouer sight did sowe therin. If ought
seme changed (sayth he) or not all togither agreing wythe
the greke/let the finder of the fawte/consyder the hebrew
phrase or maner of speche lefte in the greek wordis &c.

Joye. So that T[indale]. in his translacion/yf any fawt
be fownde/wolde seme to flitte from Greek to hebrew/from
the present tence to the future/from persone to persone/
from nowmber to number/yea and as yt playnely i. pe. 4.
apereth in altering the texte of Peter/and in altering these
sayd places from the latyn texte/euen clene from the trwthe
of the texte vnto hys owne vayne imaginacions/as euery
reder maye wel perceyue. If he were so wel sene in the
greek as he maketh him selfe/doing siche diligence in this
his correccion as he pretendeth and professeth/he shulde
haue lefte out some of so many vayne and fryuole notis in
the mergent nothing corresponding nor expowning the texte/
and haue mended mo fawtes in his texte/At the firste opening
of his boke/I chaunced vpon this glose in the i. ioan. 3
mergent. Loue is the firste precept and cause of all other.
And I loked on the tother syde/and there I sawe ageinst yt
this other: Fayth is the firste commandment and loue the
seconde/whych gloses (except T[indale]. geue vs the thirde
glose to declare and conciliate these two) maye apere contrarye to the reders: how be it methinketh yt not good so
derkely and doutefully to glose where the text is playne/
that we must go make glose vpon glose/and so at laste lede

men from the texte to wander in gloses as it hath bene in tymes paste: and paraduenture Tin[dale]. wolde haue geuen vs the thirde glose to/had the mergent haue ben able to receyue yt for other gloses/gloses/and al lytel to the pur-

Mat. 1   pose. I meruel that aftir T[indale]. in his first translacion our ladie was maryed vnto Joseph/and that now in his new correccion she is but betrouthed to him. If his first translacion were trwe in this place/why then did he correck it? And yf it were false that she was maryed to Joseph when she was there espyed grete with childe/how shall we proue that crist was conceyued in wedlok: which thynge Matthews

luc. 1   mynde is there to proue yt/and luke affirmeth the same/the worde translated into this latyne worde *desponsata*/ which worde aftir my pore lerning/by the reson of the pre posicion/*De*/in composicion signifyeth more then the simple worde *sponsata*/and maketh the verbe to bere wyth yt more encrease and fulnes. Also this sentence in latyne folowing/ *priusquam congressi fuissent*/Tin[dale]. englesshith/before they came to dwell togither: in which whether he hath translated trwly the mynde of th[e]euangelist let the lerned in cristis chirche be iuges. I wolde haue thus translated it. When Mary/his mother was maryed vnto Joseph/before they had layne togither/she was espyed to be with chylde: which was by the holy goste. For she was saluted in wedlok and conceiued criste by the holy goste/before she knew (that is) slept with hir howsbonde/as the order of the text and story tolde/declareth.

When T[indale]. hath mended these fautes/I shal shewe him moo. And for al his grete diligence in adding the pistles of the olde Testament/yet hath he missed the kushen in many placis/and must be compelled to mende hys fawtis aftir myn ensample/orels leue the reder as yt were in hys Maze sekyng for some of the pistles where he shal neuer finde them.

Paulis mynde is that. ii. or. iij. one aftir a nother
1. cor. 14.   (thoughe Tin[dale]. translateth two at once or thre at once contrary to the text) may interprete scriptures in the chirche/wother men iuging and tryinge their interpretacions by the scriptures. And if aught be reueled and geuen to any other that sitteth bye and hereth the firste/the first man shulde holde his peace and here him/

and not euen anon to wryte any maliciouse and contenciouse pistle agenst him / as dothe T[indale] agenst me. Paule commandeth vs to do al thingis for the edifying and consolacion of the chirche / and not to destroye / auerte / confounde / and inquyet yt as hath T[indale]. done by his sclaunderouse and sediciouse pistle. The mynde and sence of one interpretour / sayth paule / is subiecte vnto a nother interpretour / him to expende and iuge yt by scriptures faythfully and louingly / and shal not T[indale's]. interpretacion be then subiecte and iuged by wother men ? will he not suffer a nother man to correcke and mende his fawtis ? but anon must break forthe into raging and lying / writing so sclaunderouse and shamelesse a pistle vpon his brother that so wel deserueth vpon his worke ? And yf he be so blindely affeccionated as euery man is / with out the more grace vnto his owne werkis and sentence : yet ought he not to auenge himselfe on this maner / so sodenly and headely casting sich confusion into amonge the congregacion / For god is not the autor of confusion but of peace &c. And euen here / by this same troublouse touche of T[indale]. may euery indifferent reder se which of vs stode on the trwe parte / whether yt was I / in translating that worde other wyse then he did / or whether yt was he aftir warde euen continently in wryting so sclaunderouse and venomouse a pistle declaring vnto all indifferent godly and not affeccionated reders of what spirit the man was caryed.

But god geue him a better mynde / and vs bothe grace to forgeue eche other / to represse al siche carnall affectis that we may be bothe reuiued and renewed with the spirit of peace and loue / that our spiritis departed from our bodis might liue with crist in heuen vntyl our bodyes aftir that sleape in the duste be awakened with the trompet of god / and resumed of our soulis to ryse and come forthe togither into that gloriouse lyfe and ioyouse glorye / perpetually to prayse and magnifye our father by hys sonne our sauiour in the holy gost / vnto whom be glorie and prayse for euer Amen.

Tindale verely might neuer abyde yt / that I especially (whether he so thynketh of wother men god knoweth) shuld translate / wryte / or medle wyth the scriptures / as thoughe the holy goste with hys giftis were restrayned vnto onely Tin[dale]. and might not breath where him listeth / as though Tin[dale]. were lerned onely / and none but he. wherefore let euery reder be warned and taught at this ensample and greuouse tentacion of this man (for I take yt no nother wyse) lest as Paule saith / we be puft vp with coninge voyd al charite which edifieth. Let vs not stonde to highly in our own opinion / lest whyle we apere lerned / we proue our self foles / and while we seme to stond faste / we lye groueling on the grownde gnawing the erthe / eting and deuowering our cristen brothers name and fame / besmering and dawbing eche other with dirte and myer.

But had it bene my enimye that thus had vniustely reuyled and vexed me / I coulde haue borne him / And yf my hater had thus oppressed me / I coude haue had avoyded hym. But yt was thou my nowne felowe / my companion in lyke perel and persecucion / my familiare / so well knowne / vnto whom I committed solouingly my secretis / with whom gladly I went into the house of god. wherefore me thynketh he shulde haue ether borne and winked at the calling of this worde *Resurrectio* the lyfe aftir this / sith yt so signifyeth / or haue paciently aboden wother mennis iugement / rather then wyth so

Psal. 55

sclanderes a pistle / so sodenly to haue rente and torne
my name with so perpetual an Infamye and
with so many fayned lyes. whiche
all God forgeue the man as I
wolde be forgeuen my
nown selfe.
Amen.

The. xxvij. daye of Februarye.

A List of WORKS

Edited by

Professor EDWARD ARBER

F.S.A.; *Fellow of King's College, London;* Hon. *Member of the Virginia and Wisconsin Historical Societies; late English Examiner at the London University; and also at the Victoria University, Manchester;* Emeritus *Professor of English Language and Literature, Mason College, Birmingham.*

An English Garner
English Reprints
The War Library
The English Scholar's Library
The first Three English Books on America
The first English New Testament, 1526
The Paston Letters, 1422-1509. Edited by JAMES GAIRDNER. 3 Vols.
A List of 837 London Publishers, 1553-1640

All the Works in this Catalogue are published at net prices

ARCHIBALD CONSTABLE AND CO.
14 PARLIAMENT ST., WESTMINSTER

NOTE

THE ENGLISH GARNER, THE ENGLISH REPRINTS, *and* THE ENGLISH SCHOLAR'S LIBRARY *are now issued in a new style of binding. A few copies in the old style are still to be had, and will be supplied if specially ordered, as long as the stock lasts. Some of Professor Arber's Publications can still be supplied on large paper. Prices on application to the Booksellers or from the Publishers.*

ARCHIBALD CONSTABLE & CO.

An English Garner.

INGATHERINGS FROM OUR HISTORY AND LITERATURE.

⁎ *Abridged Lists of the Texts; many of which are very rare and not obtainable in any other form.*

VOL. I.
Small Paper.   Cloth, 5s. net.

English Political, Naval, and Military History, etc. etc.

1. The Expedition to Scotland in May 1543.
2. R. PEEKE'S fight at Xerez with a quarter-staff against Three Spaniards at once, armed with poniards and daggers: when he killed one and put the other two to flight. 1625.
3. The capture of Cris in Galatia by Captain QUAILE and 35 men. 1626.
4. Ranks in the British Army, about 1630.
5. The Return of CHARLES II. to Whitehall, 1660.
6. The Retaking of St. Helena, 1673.

English Voyages, Travels, Commerce, etc. etc.

7. The Beginnings of English Trade with the Levant, 1511-1570.
8. The Voyage from Lisbon to Goa of the first Englishman [THOMAS STEVENS, a Jesuit] known to have reached India by the Cape of Good Hope. 1572.
9. The extraordinary Captivity, for 19 years, of Captain ROBERT KNOX in Ceylon; with his singular deliverance. 1660-1679.

English Life and Progress

10. The Benefits of observing Fish Days. 1594.
11. The Great Frost. Cold doings in London. 1608.
12. The Carriers of London and the Inns they stopped at in 1637.
13. A Narrative of the Draining of the Fens. 1661.

English Literature, Literary History, and Biography.

14. Sir HENRY SIDNEY. A Letter to his son PHILIP when at Shrewsbury School.

English Poetry.

15. Love Posies. Collected about 1590.
16. Sir PHILIP SIDNEY. ASTROPHEL and STELLA [Sonnets] 1591. With the story of his affection for Lady PENELOPE DEVEREUX, afterwards RICH.
17. EDMUND SPENSER *and others.* ASTROPHEL. A Pastoral Elegy on Sir PHILIP SIDNEY. 1591.
18. JOHN DENNIS. The Secrets of Angling [*i.e. Trout Fishing*]. 1613. Forty years before WALTON'S *Angler*.
19. Many other single Poems by various Authors.

An English Garner.

VOL. II.

Small Paper.   *Cloth, 5s. net.*

English Political, Naval, and Military History, etc. etc.

1. The Triumph at Calais and Boulogne of HENRY VIII. [with ANNE BOLEYN] and FRANCIS I. November 1532.
2. The Coronation Procession of Queen ANNE [BOLEYN] from the Tower through London to Westminster. June 1533.
3. English Army Rations in 1591.
4. Rev. T. PRINCE. A History of New England in the form of Annals, from 1602 to 1633. Published at Boston, N.E., in 1736-1755. This is the most exact condensed account in existence of the foundation of our first Colonies in America.

English Voyages, Travels, Commerce, etc. etc.

5. Captain T. SANDERS. The unfortunate voyage of the *Jesus* to Tripoli, where the crew were made slaves. 1584-1585.
6. N. H. The Third Circumnavigation of the Globe, by THOMAS CAVENDISH, in the *Desire*. 1586-1588.
7. The famous fight of the *Dolphin* against Five Turkish Men-of-War off Cagliari. 1617.

English Life and Progress.

8. Dr. J. DEE. The Petty Navy Royal. [Fisheries.] 1577.
9. Captain HITCHCOCK. A Political Plat [*Scheme*], etc. [Herring Fisheries.]
10. D. DEFOE. The Education of Women. 1692.

English Literature, Literary History, and Biography.

11. F. MERES. A Sketch of English Literature, etc., up to September 1598. This is the most important contemporary account of SHAKESPEARE'S Works to this date; including some that have apparently perished.
12. J. WRIGHT. The Second Generation of English Actors. 1625-1670. This includes some valuable information respecting London Theatres during this period.

English Poetry.

13. Sir P. SIDNEY. Sonnets and Poetical Translations. Before 1587.
14. H. CONSTABLE, *and others*. DIANA. [Sonnets.] 1594.
15. Madrigals, Elegies, and Poems, by various other Poets.

An English Garner.

VOL. III.
Small Paper. Cloth, 5s. net.

English Political, Naval, and Military History, etc. etc.

1. W. PATTEN. The Expedition into Scotland: with the Battle of Pinkie Cleugh or Musselburgh, 1547. This was the 'Rough Wooing of MARY, Queen of Scots,' whom the English wanted to marry EDWARD VI.

English Voyages, Travels, Commerce, etc. etc.

2. J. H. VAN LINSCHOTEN. Voyage to Goa and back, in Portugese carracks. 1583-1592.
This work showed the way to the East, and led to the formation of the Dutch and the English East India Companies. For nearly three years this Dutchman, returning in charge of a cargo of pepper, spices, etc., was pinned up in the Azores by the English ships; of whose daring deeds he gives an account.

3. E. WRIGHT. The voyage of the Earl of CUMBERLAND to the Azores in 1589. This is a part of LINSCHOTEN'S story re-told more fully from an English point of view.

4. The first Englishmen—JOHN NEWBERY and RALPH FITCH—that ever reached India overland, *viâ* Aleppo and the Persian Gulf, in 1583-1589. They met with LINSCHOTEN there; and also T. Stevens the Jesuit, see vol. i. p. 130.

English Life and Progress.

5. J. CAIUS, M.D. Of English Dogs. 1536. Translated from the Latin by A. FLEMING in 1576.

6. Britain's Buss. A Computation of the Cost and Profit of a Herring Buss or Ship. 1615.

English Literature, Literary History, and Biography.

7. T. ELLWOOD. Relations with J. MILTON. This young Quaker rendered many services to the Poet; amongst which was the suggestion of *Paradise Regained*.

8. J. DRYDEN. Of Dramatic Poesy. An Essay. This charming piece of English Prose was written in 1665 and published in 1668. With it is given the entire Controversy between DRYDEN and Sir R. HOWARD on this subject.

English Poetry.

9. S. DANIEL. DELIA. [Sonnets.] 1594.
10. T. CAMPION, M.D. Songs and Poems. 1601-1613.
11. Lyrics, Elegies, etc., by other Poets.

An English Garner.

VOL. IV.
Small Paper. Cloth, 5s. net.

English Political, Naval, and Military History, etc. etc.

1. E. UNDERHILL 'the Hot Gospeller' Imprisonment in 1553, with Anecdotes of Queen MARY's Coronation Procession, WYATT's Rebellion, the Marriage of PHILIP and MARY, etc.
2. J. FOX. The Imprisonment of the Princess ELIZABETH. 1554-1555.
3. Texts relating to the Winning of Calais and Guisnes by the French in January 1556.
4. The Coronation Procession of Queen ELIZABETH. January 1559.
5. Sir THOMAS OVERBURY. Observations of Holland, Flanders, and France in 1609. A most sagacious Political Study.
6. JAMES I. The Book of Sports. 1618.
7. Abp. G. ABBOTT. Narrative of his Sequestration from Office in 1627 by CHARLES I., at the instigation of BUCKINGHAM and LAUD.
8. Major-General Sir T. MORGAN. Progress [*i.e. March*] in France and Flanders with the 6000 'Red Coats' at the taking of Dunkirk, etc., in 1657-8.

English Voyages, Travels, Commerce, etc. etc.

9. The first Britons who ever reached the city of Mexico: T. BLAKE, a Scotchman, before 1536; and J. FIELD and R. TOMSON, 1556.
10. The wonderful Recovery of the *Exchange* from forty-five Turkish pirates of Algiers by J. RAWLINS and twenty-four other slaves. February 1622.

English Life and Progress.

11. T. GENTLEMAN. England's Way to Win Wealth. [Fisheries.] The Dutch obtained more wealth from their Herring Fishery *along the English shores* than the Spaniards did from their American gold mines.

English Poetry.

12. ? T. OCCLEVE. The Letter of CUPID. 1402.
13. L. SHEPHERD. JOHN BON and Mast[er] PARSON. [A Satire on the Mass.] 1551.
14. Rev. T. BRICE. A Register of the Tormented and Cruelly Burned within England. 1555-1558. These verses give the names of most of the Marian Martyrs.
15. J. C. ALCILIA; PHILOPARTHEN's loving folly! [Love Poems.] 1595.
16. G. WITHER. Fair VIRTUE, the Mistress of PHIL'ARETE. 1622. This is WITHER's masterpiece. Over 6000 lines of verse in many metrical forms.
17. The Songs that JOHN DOWLAND, the famous Lutenist, set to music.

An English Garner.

VOL. V.
Small Paper. Cloth, 5s. net.

English Political, Naval, and Military History, etc. etc.

1. J. SAVILE, King JAMES's Entertainment at Theobalds, and his Welcome to London. 1603.
2. G. DUGDALE. The Time Triumphant. King JAMES's Coronation at Westminster, 25 July 1603; and Coronation Procession [delayed by the Plague], 15 March 1604.

English Voyages, Travels, Commerce, etc. etc.

3. The Voyages to Brazil of WILLIAM HAWKINS, Governor of Plymouth and father of Sir JOHN, about 1530.
4. Sir J. HAWKINS. First Voyage to the West Indies, 1562-1563. This was the beginning of the English Slave Trade.
5. R. BODENHAM. A Trip to Mexico. 1564-1565.
6. Sir J. HAWKINS. Second Voyage to the West Indies. 1564-1565.
7. Sir J. HAWKINS. Third and disastrous Voyage to the West Indies, 1567-1569: with the base treachery of the Spaniards at San Juan de Ulna, near Vera Cruz; and the extraordinary adventures of Three of the Survivors. This was DRAKE's 2nd Voyage to the West Indies; and the first in which he commanded a ship, the *Judith*.
8. Sir F. DRAKE's 3rd (1570), 4th (1571), and 5th (1572-73), Voyages to the West Indies. Especially the 5th, known as The Voyage to Nombre de Dios: in which, on 11 February 1573, he first saw the Pacific Ocean; and then besought GOD to give him life to sail once in an English ship on that sea. [See opposite page.]

English Life and Progress.

9. B. FRANKLIN. 'Poor Richard' improved. Proverbs of Thrift and to discourage useless expense. Philadelphia, 1757.

English Poetry.

10. B. BARNES. PARTHENOPHIL and PARTHENOPHE. Sonnets, Madrigals, Elegies and Odes. 1593. [A perfect Storehouse of Versification, including the only *treble* Sestine in our language.]
11. ZEPHERIA. [Canzons.] 1594.
12. Sir J. DAVIES. Orchestra or a Poem on Dancing. 1596.
13. B. GRIFFIN. FIDESSA, more chaste than kind. [Sonnets.] 1596.
14. Sir J. DAVIES. *Nosce teipsum!* In two Elegies: (1) Of Human Knowledge, (2) Of the Soul of Man and the Immortality thereof. 1599.
15. Sir J. DAVIES. Hymns of ASTRÆA [*i.e.* Queen ELIZABETH.] In acrostic verse. 1599.

VOL. VI.
Small Paper.   Cloth, 5s. net.

English Political, Naval, and Military History, etc. etc.

1. The Examination, at Saltwood Castle, Kent, of WILLIAM of THORPE by Abp. T. ARUNDELL, 7 August 1407.   Edited by W. TYNDALE, 1530.   This is the best account of Lollardism from the inside, given by one who was the leader of the second generation of Lollards.

English Voyages, Travels, Commerce, etc. etc.

2. J. CHILTON.   Travels in Mexico.   1568-1575.
3. J. BION.   An Account of the Torments, etc.   1708.

English Life and Progress.

4. The most dangerous Adventure of R. FERRIS, A. HILL, and W. THOMAS; who went in a boat by sea from London to Bristol.   1590.
5. Leather.   A Discourse to Parliament.   1629.
6. H. PEACHAM.   The Worth of a Penny, or a Caution to keep Money.   1641.   With all the variations of the later Editions.
7. Sir W. PETTY.   Political Arithmetic.   [Written in 1677.]   1690.   One of the earliest and best books on the Science of Wealth.

English Literature, Literary History, and Biography.

8. ISAAC BICKERSTAFF, Esq.   [Dean J. Swift.]   Predictions for the year 1708.   [One of these was the death of J. PARTRIDGE, the *Almanack* Maker, on 29 March 1708.]   Other Tracts of this laughable controversy follow.
9. [J. GAY.]   The Present State of Wit.   3 May 1711.   [A Survey of our Periodical Literature at this date; including the *Review*, *Tatler*, and *Spectator*.]
10. [Dr. J. ARBUTHNOT.]   Law [*i.e. War*] is a Bottomless Pit, exemplified in the Case of the Lord STRUTT [*the Kings of Spain*], JOHN BULL [*England*] the Clothier, NICHOLAS FROG [*Holland*] the Linendraper, and LEWIS BABOON [LOUIS XIV. of Bourbon = *France*].   In Four Parts.   1712.
This famous Political Satire on the War of the Spanish Succession was designed to prepare the English public for the Peace of Utrecht, signed on 11 April 1713.   In part I., on 28 February 1712, first appeared in our Literature, the character of JOHN BULL for an Englishman.
11. T. TICKELL.   The life of ADDISON.   1721.
12. Sir R. STEELE.   Epistle to W. CONGREVE [in reply.]   1722.

English Poetry.

13. The first printed *Robin Hood* Ballad.   Printed about 1510.
14. W. PERCY.   COELIA.   [Sonnets.]   1594.
15. G. WITHER.   FIDELIA.   [This is WITHER'S second masterpiece.   The Lament of a Woman thinking that she is forsaken in love.]   1615.
16. M. DRAYTON.   IDEA.   [Sonnets.]   1619.
17. The Interpreter.   [A Political Satire interpreting the meaning of The Protestant, The Puritan, The Papist.]   1622.

An English Garner. 7

VOL. VII.
Small Paper.   Cloth, 5s. net.

English Political, Naval, and Military History, etc. etc.

1. Sir F. VERE, *General of the English troops in the Dutch service..* Commentaries of his Services: at (1) the Storming of Cadiz in 1596, (2) the Action at Turnhout in 1597 (3) The Battle of Nieuport in 1600: but especially (4) the Siege of Ostend, of which place he was Governor from 11 June 1601 to 7 June 1602.
2. The Retaking of *The Friends' Adventure* from the French by R. LYDE and a boy. 1693.

English Voyages, Travels, Commerce, etc. etc.

3. H. PITMAN. Relation, etc. For doing noble Red Cross work at the Battle of Sedgemoor; this Surgeon was sent as a White Slave to Barbadoes, etc. 1689.

English Life and Progress.

4. W. KEMP's [SHAKESPEARE'S fellow Actor] Nine Days Wonder; performed in a Morris Dance from London to Norwich. April 1600.
5. A series of Texts on the indignities offered to the Established Clergy, and especially the Private Chaplains, in the Restoration Age, by the Royalist laity; including
Dr. J. EACHARD'S witty 'Grounds of the Contempt of the Clergy and Religion.' 1670.

English Literature, Literary History, and Biography.

6. Another Series of Tracts, in prose and verse, illustrating the great Public Services rendered by D. DEFOE, up to the death of Queen Anne; including:
   D. DEFOE.   An Appeal to Honour and Justice, etc.   1715.
   D. DEFOE.   The *True* Born Englishman.   1701.
   D. DEFOE.   The History of *Kentish Petition.*   1701.
   D. DEFOE.   LEGION'S *Memorial.*   1701.
   D. DEFOE.   The Shortest Way with the Dissenters, etc.   1702.
   D. DEFOE.   A Hymn to the Pillory.   1703.
   D. DEFOE.   Prefaces to the *Review.*   1704-1710.

English Poetry.

7. T. DELONEY.   Three Ballads on the Armada fight.   August 1588.
8. R. L.   (1) DIELLA [Sonnets]; (2) The Love of Dom DIEGO and GYNEURA. 1596.
9. AN. SC. DAIPHHANTUS, or the Passions of Love.   1604.
See also above.
   D. DEFOE.   The *True* Born Englishman.   1701.
   D. DEFOE.   A Hymn to the Pillory.   1703.

An English Garner.

VOL. VIII.
Small Paper. Cloth, 5s. net.

This Index Volume will, if possible, contain the following:—

English Political, Naval, and Military History, etc. etc.

1. J. PROCTOR. The History of WYATT's Rebellion. 1554.
2. The burning of Paul's Church, London. 1568.
3. G. GASCOIGNE the Poet. The Spanish Fury at Antwerp. 1577.
4. J. LINGHAM. English Captains in the Low Countries. 1584.
5. The Burial of MARY QUEEN of Scots at Peterborough Cathedral. 1 August 1587.
6. T. M. The Entertainment of JAMES I. from Edinburgh to London. 1603.
7. Bp. W. BARLOW. The Hampton Court Conference. 1604.
8. The Speeches in the Star Chamber at the Censure of BASTWICK, BARTON, and PRYNNE. 1637.
9. N. N. The Expedition of the Prince of ORANGE. 1688.

English Voyages, Travels, Commerce, etc. etc.

10. The strange things that happened to R. HASLETON in his ten years Travels. 1585-1595.
11. E. PELLHAM. The miraculous Deliverence of eight Englishmen left in Greenland, anno 1630, nine months and twelve days.

English Life and Progress.

12. J. MAY. The Estate of Clothing [*the manufacture of woollen Cloths*] now in England. 1613.

English Poetry.

13. A translation [? by Sir E. DYER] of Six of the Idyllia of THEOCRITUS. 1588.
14. Verses penned by D. GWIN, eleven years a slave in the Spanish galleys, and presented by him to Queen ELIZABETH on 18 August 1588.
15. W. SMITH. CHLORIS. [Sonnets.] 1596.
16. T. STORER. The Life and Death of Cardinal WOLSEY. 1599.
17. E. W. Thameseidos. In 3 Cantos. 1600.
18. Some Collections of Posies. 1624-1679.

Chronological List of Works included in the Series.

Index.

English Reprints.

No.		Text.		s.	d.
1.	Milton	*Areopagitica*	1644	1	0
2.	Latimer	*The Ploughers*	1549	1	0
3.	Gosson	*The School of Abuse*	1579	1	0
4.	Sidney	*An Apology for Poetry*	? 1580	1	0
5.	E. Webbe	*Travels*	1590	1	0
6.	Selden	*Table Talk*	1634-54	1	0
7.	Ascham	*Toxophilus*	1544	1	0
8.	Addison	*Criticism on* Paradise Lost	1711-12	1	0
9.	Lyly	EUPHUES	1579-80	4	0
10.	Villiers	*The Rehearsal*	1671	1	0
11.	Gascoigne	*The Steel Glass, etc.*	1576	1	0
12.	Earle	*Micro-cosmographie*	1628	1	0
13.	Latimer	7 *Sermons before* EDWARD VI.	1549	1	6
14.	More	*Utopia*	1516-57	1	0
15.	Puttenham	*The Art of English Poesy*	1589	2	6
16.	Howell	*Instructions for Foreign Travel*	1642	1	0
17.	Udall	*Roister Doister*	1553-66	1	0
18.	Mk. of Eves.	*The Revelation, etc.*	1186-1410	1	0
19.	James I.	*A Counterblast to Tobacco, etc.*	1604	1	0
20.	Naunton	*Fragmenta Regalia*	1653	1	0
21.	Watson	*Poems*	1582-93	1	6
22.	Habington	CASTARA	1640	1	0
23.	Ascham	*The Schoolmaster*	1570	1	0
24.	Tottel's	*Miscellany* [Songs and Sonnets]	1557	2	6
25.	Lever	*Sermons*	1550	1	0
26.	W. Webbe	*A Discourse of English Poetry*	1586	1	0
27.	Lord Bacon	A Harmony of the *Essays*	1597-1626	5	0
28.	Roy, etc.	*Read me, and be not wroth!*	1528	1	6
29.	Raleigh, etc.	*Last Fight of the 'Revenge'*	1591	1	0
30.	Googe	*Eglogues, Epitaphs, and Sonnets*	1563	1	0
				41	6

(For full titles, etc., see pp. 11-20.)

1.
JOHN MILTON.

Areopagitica.
1644.

(*a*) AREOPAGITICA: *A Speech of Mr.* JOHN MILTON *For the Liberty of Vnlicenc'd Printing, To the Parliament of England.*

(*b*) A Decree of Starre-Chamber, concerning Printing, made the eleuenth of July last past, 1637.

(*c*) An Order of the Lords and Commons assembled in Parliament for the Regulating of Printing, &c. 1643.

LORD MACAULAY. He attacked the licensing system in that sublime treatise which every statesman should wear as a sign upon his hand, and as frontlets between his eyes.—*Edinburgh Review, p.* 344, *August* 1825.

H. HALLAM. Many passages in this famous tract are admirably eloquent: an intense love of liberty and truth flows through it: the majestic soul of MILTON breathes such high thoughts as had not been uttered before.—*Introduction to the Literature of Europe,* iii. 66a. *Ed.* 1839.

W. H. PRESCOTT. The most splendid argument, perhaps, the world had then witnessed on behalf of intellectual liberty.—*History of* FERDINAND *and* ISABELLA, iii. 391. *Ed.* 1845.

2.
HUGH LATIMER.
Ex-Bishop of Worcester.

The Ploughers.
1549.

A notable Sermon of ye reuerende father Master HUGHE LATIMER, *whiche he preached in ye Shrouds at paules churche in London on the xviii daye of Januarye.*

SIR R. MORISON. Did there ever any one (I say not in England only, but among other nations) flourish since the time of the Apostles; who preached the gospel more sincerely, purely, and honestly, than HUGH LATIMER, Bishop of Worcester.—*Apomaxis Calumniarum . . quibus* JOANNES COCLEUS *&c.,* f. 78. *Ed.* 1537.

It was in this Sermon, that LATIMER (himself an ex-Bishop) astonished his generation, by saying that the Devil was the most diligent Prelate and Preacher in all England. "Ye shal neuer fynde him idle I warraunte you."

3.
STEPHEN GOSSON.
Stud. Oxon.

The School of Abuse.
1579.

(*a*) *The Schoole of Abuse. Conteining a pleasaunt inuectiue against Poets, Pipers, Plaiers, Jesters, and such like Caterpillers of a Common wealth; Setting vp the Flagge of Defiance to their mischieuous exercise, and ouerthrowing their Bulwarkes, by Prophane Writers, Naturall reason and common experience.*

1579.

(*b*) *An Apologie of the Schoole of Abuse, against Poets, Pipers, Players, and their Excusers.* [*Dec.*]

1579.

∴ This attack is thought to have occasioned Sir PHILIP SIDNEY'S writing of the following *Apologie for Poesie.*

GOSSON was, in succession, Poet, Actor, Dramatist, Satirist, and a Puritan Clergyman.

4.
Sir PHILIP SIDNEY.

An Apology for Poetry.
[? 1580.]

An Apologie for Poetrie. Written by the right noble, vertuous, and learned Sir PHILIP SIDNEY, *Knight.* 1595.

H. W. LONGFELLOW. The defence of Poetry is a work of rare merit. It is a golden little volume, which the scholar may lay beneath his pillow, as CHRYSOSTOM did the works of ARISTOPHANES. — *North American Review, p.* 57. *January* 1832.

The Work thus divides itself:
The Etymology of Poetry.
The Anatomy of the Effects of Poetry.
The Anatomy of the Parts of Poetry.
Objections to Poetry answered.
Criticism of the existing English Poetry.

5.
EDWARD WEBBE.
A Chief Master Gunner.

Travels.
1590.

The rare and most vvonderful thinges which EDWARD WEBBE *an Englishman borne, hath seene and passed in his troublesome trauailes, in the Citties of Ierusalem, Damasko, Bethelem and Galely: and in all the landes of Iewrie, Egipt, Grecia, Russia, and in the Land of Prester John. Wherein is set foorth his extreame slauerie sustained many yeres togither, in the Gallies and wars of the great Turk against the Landes of Persia, Tartaria, Spaine, and Portugall, with the manner of his releasement and coming to England.* [1590.]

6.
JOHN SELDEN.

Table Talk.
[1634-1654.]

Table Talk: being the Discourses of JOHN SELDEN, *Esq.; or his Sence of various Matters of weight and high consequence, relating especially to Religion and State.* 1689.

S. T. COLERIDGE. There is more weighty bullion sense in this book than I ever found in the same number of pages of any uninspired writer. . . . O! to have been with SELDEN over his glass of wine, making every accident an outlet and a vehicle of wisdom.—*Literary Remains,* iii. 361-2. *Ed.* 1836.

H. HALLAM. This very short and small volume gives, perhaps, a more exalted notion of SELDEN's natural talents than any of his learned writings. — *Introduction to the Literature of Europe,* iii. 347. *Ed.* 1836.

Above all things, Liberty!

7.
ROGER ASCHAM.

Toxophilus.
1544.

Toxophilus, the Schole of Shootinge, conteyned in two bookes.
To all Gentlemen and yomen of Englande, pleasaunte for theyr pastime to rede, and profitable for theyr use to follow both in war and peace.

In a dialogue between TOXOPHILUS and PHILOEOGUS, ASCHAM not only gives us one of the very best books on Archery in our language; but as he tells King Henry VIII., in his Dedication, "this litle treatise was purposed, begon, and ended of me, onelie for this intent, that Labour, Honest pastime, and Vertu might recouer againe that place and right, that Idlenesse, Unthriftie Gaming, and Vice hath put them fro."

8.
JOSEPH ADDISON.

Criticism on *Paradise Lost.*
1711-1712.

From the *Spectator*, being its Saturday issues between 31 December, 1711, and 3 May 1712. In these papers, which constitute a Primer to *Paradise Lost*, ADDISON first made known and interpreted, to the general English public, the great Epic poem, which had then been published nearly half-a-century.

After a general discussion of the *Fable*, the *Characters*, the *Sentiments*, the *Language*, and the *Defects* of MILTON's Great Poem; the Critic devotes a Paper to the consideration of the *Beauties* of each of its Twelve Books.

9.
JOHN LYLY,
Novelist, Wit, Poet, and Dramatist.

Euphues.
1579-1580.

EUPHVES, *the Anatomy of Wit. Very pleasant for all Gentlemen to reade, and most necessary to remember.*

VVherein are conteined the delights that Wit followeth in his youth, by the pleasantnesse of loue, and the happinesse he reapeth in age by the perfectnesse of Wisedome.
1579.
EUPHUES *and his England. Containing his voyage and aduentures, myxed with sundry pretie discourses of honest Loue, the description of the countrey, the Court, and the manners of that Isle.*
1580.

Of great importance in our Literary History.

10.

GEORGE VILLIERS,
Second Duke of BUCK-INGHAM.

The Rehearsal.
1671.

The Rehearsal, as it was Acted at the Theatre Royal.

Many of the passages of anterior plays that were parodied in this famous Dramatic Satire on DRYDEN in the character of *BAYES*, are placed on opposite pages to the text. BRIAN FAIRFAX's remarkable life of this Duke of BUCKINGHAM is also prefixed to the play.

The Heroic Plays, first introduced by Sir W. D'AVENANT, and afterwards greatly developed by DRYDEN, are the object of this laughable attack. LACY, who acted the part of *BAYES*, imitated the dress and gesticulation of DRYDEN.
The Poet repaid this compliment to the Duke of BUCKINGHAM, in 1681, by introducing him in the character of ZIMRI in his *ABSOLOM and ACHITOPHEL*.

11.

GEORGE GASCOIGNE,
Soldier and Poet.

The Steel Glass, &c.
1576.

(*a*) *A Remembraunce of the wel imployed life, and godly end, of* GEORGE GASKOIGNE, *Esquire, who deceassed at Stalmford in Lincoln shire, the* 7 *of October,* 1577. *The reporte of* GEOR. WHETSTONS, *Gent.* [1577.]
There is only one copy of this metrical Life. It is in the Bodleian Library.

(*b*) *Certayne notes of instruction concerning the making of verse or ryme in English.* 1575.
This is our First printed piece of Poetical Criticism.

(*c*) *The Steele Glas.*
Written in Blank Verse. Probably the fourth printed English Satire: those by BARCLAY, ROY, and Sir T. WYATT being the three earlier ones.

(*d*) *The Complaynt of* PHILOMENE. *An Elegie.* 1576.

12.

JOHN EARLE,
Afterwards Bishop of SALISBURY.

Microcosmographie.
1628.

Micro-cosmographie, or a Peece of the World discovered; in Essays and Characters.

This celebrated book of Characters is graphically descriptive of the English social life of the time, as it presented itself to a young Fellow of Merton College, Oxford; including *A She precise Hypocrite, A Sceptic in Religion, A good old man,* &c.

This Work is a notable specimen of a considerable class of books in our Literature, full of interest; and which help Posterity much better to understand the Times in which they were written.

13.
HUGH LATIMER,
Ex-Bishop of WORCESTER.

Seven Sermons before Edward VI.
1549.

The fyrste [—*seuenth*] *Sermon of Mayster* HUGHE LATIMER, *whiche he preached before the Kynges Maiestie wythin his graces palayce at Westminster on each Friday in Lent.*
1549.

Sir JAMES MACKINTOSH. LATIMER, . . brave, sincere, honest, inflexible, not distinguished as a writer or a scholar, but exercising his power over men's minds by a fervid eloquence flowing from the deep conviction which animated his plain, pithy, and free-spoken Sermons.—*History of England*, ii. 291. *Ed.* 1831.

14.
Sir THOMAS MORE.

Translation of Utopia.
1516-1557.

A frutefull and pleasaunt worke of the best state of a publique weale, and of the new yle called Utopia: VVritten in Latine by Sir THOMAS MORE *Knyght, and translated into Englyshe by* RALPH ROBYNSON.

Lord CAMPBELL. Since the time of PLATO, there had been no composition given to the world which, for imagination, for philosophical discrimination, for a familiarity with the principles of government, for a knowledge of the springs of human action, for a keen observation of men and manners, and for felicity of expression, could be compared to the *Utopia.*—*Lives of the Lord Chancellors* (*Life of Sir T. More*) i. 583, *Ed.* 1845.

In the imaginary country of Utopia, MORE endeavours to sketch out a State based upon two principles—(1) community of goods, no private property; and consequently (2) no use for money.

15.
GEORGE PUTTENHAM,
A Gentleman Pensioner to Queen ELIZABETH.

The Art of English Poesy.
1589.

The Arte of English Poesie.
Contriued into three Bookes : *The first of* POETS *and* POESIE, *the second of* PROPORTION, *the third of* ORNAMENT.

W. OLDYS. It contains many pretty observations, examples, characters, and fragments of poetry for those times, now nowhere else to be met with.—*Sir* WALTER RALEIGH, liv. *Ed.* 1736.

O. GILCHRIST. On many accounts one of the most curious and entertaining, and intrinsically one of the most valuable, books of the age of QUEEN ELIZABETH. The copious intermixture of contemporary anecdote, tradition, manners, opinions, and the numerous specimens of coeval poetry nowhere else preserved, contribute to form a volume of infinite amusement, curiosity, and value.—*Censura Literaria*, i. 339. *Ed.* 1805.

This is still also an important book on Rhetoric and the Figures of Speech.

16.
JAMES HOWELL,
Clerk of the Council to CHARLES I.; *afterwards Historiographer to* CHARLES II.

Instructions for Foreign Travel.
1642.

Instructions for forreine travell. Shewing by what cours, and in what compasse of time, one may take an exact Survey of the Kingdomes and States of Christendome, and arrive to the practicall knowledge of the Languages, to good purpose.

The *MURRAY, BÆDEKER,* and *Practical Guide* to the Grand Tour of Europe, which, at that time, was considered the finishing touch to the complete education of an English Gentleman.

The route sketched out by this delightfully quaint Writer, is France, Spain, Italy, Switzerland, Germany, the Netherlands, and Holland. The time allowed is 3 years and 4 months: the months to be spent in travelling, the years in residence at the different cities.

17.
NICHOLAS UDALL,
Master, first of Eton College, then of Westminster School.

Roister Doister.
[1553-1566.]

This is believed to be the first true English Comedy that ever came to the press.

From the unique copy, which wants a title-page, now at Eton College; and which is thought to have been printed in 1566.

Dramatis Personæ.

RALPH ROISTER DOISTER.
MATTHEW MERRYGREEK.
GAWIN GOODLUCK, *affianced to Dame* CUSTANCE.
TRISTRAM TRUSTY, *his friend.*
DOBINET DOUGHTY, *"boy" to* ROISTER DOISTER.
TOM TRUEPENNY, *servant to Dame* CUSTANCE.
SIM SURESBY, *servant to* GOODLUCK.
Scrivener.
Harpax.

Dame CHRISTIAN CUSTANCE, *a widow.*
MARGERY MUMBLECRUST, *her nurse.*
TIBET TALKAPACE } *her*
ANNOT ALYFACE } *maidens*

18.
A Monk of Evesham.

The Revelation, &c.
1186[-1410]. 1485.

¶ *Here begynnyth a maruelous reuelacion that was schewyd of almighty god by sent Nycholas to a monke of Euyshamme yn the days of Kynge Richard the fyrst. And the yere of owre lord.* M.C.Lxxxxvi.

One of the rarest of English books printed by one of the earliest of English printers, WILLIAM DE MACLINIA; who printed this text about 1485, *in the lifetime of* CAXTON.

The essence of the story is as old as it professes to be; but contains later additions, the orthography being of about 1410, It is very devoutly written, and contains a curious Vision of Purgatory.

The Writer is a prototype of BUNYAN; and his description of the Gate in the Crystal Wall of Heaven, and of the solemn and marvellously sweet Peal of the Bells of Heaven that came to him through it, is very beautiful.

19.
JAMES I.

A Counter-blast to Tobacco.
1604.

(a) *The Essayes of a Prentise, in the Diuine Arte of Poesie.*

Printed while JAMES VI. of Scotland, at Edinburgh in 1585; and includes *Ane Schort treatise, conteining some Reulis and Cautelis to be obseruit and eschewit in Scottis Poesie,* which is another very early piece of printed Poetical Criticism.

(b) *A Counterblaste to Tobacco.* 1604.

To this text has been added a full account of *the Introduction and Early use of Tobacco in England.* The herb first came into use in Europe as a medicinal leaf for poultices: smoking it was afterwards learnt from the American Indians.

Our Royal Author thus sums up his opinion:
"A custome lothsome to the eye, hatefull to the nose, harmefull to the braine, dangerous to the lungs, and in the blacke stinking fume thereof, nearest resembling the horrible Stigian smoke of the pit that is bottomlesse."

20.
Sir ROBERT NAUNTON,
Master of the Court of Wards.

Fragmenta Regalia.
1653.

Fragmenta Regalia: or Observations on the late Queen ELIZABETH, *her Times and Favourites.* [1630.]

Naunton writes:
"And thus I have delivered up this my poor Essay; a little Draught of this great Princess, and her Times, with the Servants of her State and favour."

21.
THOMAS WATSON,
Londoner, Student-at-Law.

Poems.
1582-1593.

(a) *The* Ἑκατομπαθια *or Passionate Centurie of Loue. Diuided into two parts: whereof, the first expresseth the Authours sufferance in Loue: the latter, his long farewell to Loue and all his tyrannie.* 1582.

(b) MELIBŒUS, *Siue Ecloga in obitum Honoratissimi Viri Domini* FRANCISCI WALSINGHAMI. 1590.

(c) *The same translated into English, by the Author.* 1590.

(d) *The Tears of Fancie, or Loue disdained.* 1593.

From the *unique* copy, wanting *Sonnets* 9-16, in the possession of S. CHRISTIE MILLER, Esq., of Britwell.

22.
WILLIAM HABING-TON.

Castara.
1640.

CASTARA. *The third Edition. Corrected and augmented.*

CASTARA was Lady LUCY HERBERT, the youngest child of the first Lord POWIS; and these Poems were chiefly marks of affection during a pure courtship followed by a happy marriage. With these, are also Songs of Friendship, especially those referring to the Hon. GEORGE TALBOT. In addition to these Poems, there are four prose Characters; on *A Mistress, A Wife, A Friend,* and *The Holy Man.*

23.
ROGER ASCHAM.

The Schoolmaster.
1570.

The Scholemaster, or plaine and perfite way of teachyng children, to vnderstand, write, and speake, in Latin tong, but specially purposed for the priuate brynging vp of youth in Ientlemen and Noble mens houses, &c.

This celebrated Work contains the story of Lady JANE GREY'S delight in reading *PLATO,* an attack on the *Italianated* Englishman of the time, and much other information not specified in the above title.

In it, ASCHAM gives us very fully his plan of studying Languages, which may be described as *the double translation of a model book.*

24.
HENRY HOWARD, *Earl of* SURREY.
Sir THOMAS WYATT.
NICHOLAS GRIMALD.
Lord VAUX.

Tottel's Miscellany.
5 June, 1557.

Songes and Sonettes, vvritten by the right honorable Lorde HENRY HOWARD *late Earle of* SURREY, *and other.*

With 39 additional Poems from the second edition by the same printer, RICHARD TOTTEL, of 31 July, 1557.

This celebrated Collection is the First of our Poetical Miscellanies, and also the first appearance in print of any considerable number of English Sonnets.

TOTTEL in his *Address to the Reader,* says:

"That to haue wel written in verse, yea and in small parcelles, deserueth great praise, the workes of diuers Latines, Italians, and other, doe proue sufficiently. That our tong is able in that kynde to do as praiseworthely as ye rest, the honorable stile of the noble earle of Surrey, and the weightinesse of the depewitted Sir Thomas Wyat the elders verse, with seuerall graces in sondry good Englishe writers, doe show abundantly."

25.
Rev. THOMAS LEVER,
Fellow and Preacher of St John's College, Cambridge.

Sermons.
1550.

(*a*) *A fruitfull Sermon in Paules church at London in the Shroudes.*

(*b*) *A Sermon preached the fourth Sunday in Lent before the Kynges Maiestie, and his honorable Counsell.*

(*c*) *A Sermon preached at Pauls Crosse.*
1550.

These Sermons are reprinted from the original editions, which are of *extreme* rarity. They throw much light on the communistic theories of the Norfolk rebels; and the one at Paul's Cross contains a curious account of Cambridge University life in the reign of EDWARD VI.

26.
WILLIAM WEBBE,
Graduate.

A Discourse of English Poetry.
1586.

A Discourse of English Poetrie. Together with the Authors iudgement, touching the reformation of our English Verse.

Another of the early pieces of Poetical Criticism, written in the year in which SHAKESPEARE is supposed to have left Stratford for London. Only two copies of this Work are known, one of these was sold for £64.

This Work should be read with STANYHURST'S *Translation of Æneid, I.-IV.*, 1582, see p. 64. WEBBE was an advocate of English Hexameters; and here translates VIRGIL'S first two Eglogues into them. He also translates into Sapphics COLIN'S Song in the Fourth Eglogue of SPENSER'S *Shephard's Calendar.*

27.
FRANCIS BACON,
afterwards Lord VERULAM Viscount ST. ALBANS.

A Harmony of the *Essays, &c.*
1597-1626.

And after my manner, I alter ever, when I add. So that nothing is finished, till all be finished.—Sir FRANCIS BACON, 27 Feb. 1610-[11.]

(*a*) *Essayes, Religious Meditations, and Places of perswasion and disswasion.* 1597.

(*b*) *The Writings of Sir FFRANCIS BACON Knight the Kinges Sollicitor Generall in Moralitie, Policie, Historie.*

(*c*) *The Essaies of Sir FRANCIS BACON Knight, the Kings Solliciter Generall.*
1612.

(*d*) *The Essayes or Counsells, Civill and Morall of FRANCIS Lord VERULAM, Viscount ST. ALBAN.* 1625.

28.
WILLIAM ROY.
JEROME BARLOW.
Franciscan Friars.

Read me, and be not wroth!
[1528].

(a) *Rede me and be nott wrothe,*
For I saye no thynge but trothe.
I will ascende makynge my state so hye,
That my pompous honoure shall never dye.
O Caytyſe when thou thynkest least of all,
With confusion thou shalt have a fall.

This is the famous satire on Cardinal WOLSEY, and is the First English *Protestant* book ever printed, not being a portion of Holy Scripture. See *p.* 22 for the Fifth such book. The next two pieces form one book, printed by HANS LUFT, at Marburg, in 1530.

(b) *A proper dyaloge, betwene a Gentillman and a husbandman, eche complaynynge to other their miserable calamite, through the ambicion of the clergye.*

(c) *A compendious old treatyse, shewynge, how that we ought to haue the scripture in Englysshe.*

29.
Sir WALTER RALEIGH.
GERVASE MARKHAM.
J. H. VAN LINSCHOTEN.

The Last Fight of the "Revenge."
1591.

(a) *A Report of the truth of the fight about the Iles of Acores, this last la Sommer. Betwixt the* REUENGE, *one of her Maiesties Shippes, and an* ARMADA *of the King of Spaine.*
[By Sir W. RALEIGH.]

(b) *The most honorable Tragedie of Sir* RICHARD GRINUILE, *Knight.* 1595.
[By GERVASE MARKHAM.]

(c) [*The Fight and Cyclone at the Azores.*
By JAN HUYGHEN VAN LINSCHOTEN.]

Several accounts are here given of one of the most extraordinary Sea fights in our Naval History.

30.
BARNABE GOOGE.

Eglogues, Epitaphs, and Sonnets.
1563.

Eglogs, Epytaphes, and Sonettes Newly written by BARNABE GOOGE.

Three copies only known. Reprinted from the *Huth* copy.
In the prefatory *Notes of the Life and Writings of B. GOOGE*, will be found an account of the trouble he had in winning MARY DARELL for his wife.

A new Literature generally begins with imitations and translations. When this book first appeared, Translations were all the rage among the "young England" of the day. This Collection of *original* Occasional Verse is therefore the more noticeable. The Introduction gives a glimpse of the principal Writers of the time, such as the Authors of the *Mirror for Magistrates*, the Translators of SENECA's *Tragedies*, &c., and including such names as BALDWIN, BAVANDE, BLUNDESTON, NEVILLE, NORTH, NORTON, SACKVILLE, and YELVERTON.

Works in the Old Spelling.

The English Scholar's Library.

16 Parts are now published, in Cloth Boards, £2, 1s.
Any part may be obtained separately.

The general character of this Series will be gathered from the following pages:—22-28.

		s.	d.
1. WILLIAM CAXTON. **Reynard the Fox**,	. .	1	6
2. JOHN KNOX. **The First Blast of the Trumpet**,		1	6
3. CLEMENT ROBINSON and *others*. **A handful of Pleasant Delights**,	. . . . .	1	6
4. [SIMON FISH.] **A Supplication for the Beggars**,		1	6
5. [*Rev.* JOHN UDALL.] **Diotrephes**,	. . .	1	6
6. [?] **The Return from Parnassus**,	. .	1	6
7. THOMAS DECKER. **The Seven Deadly Sins of London**,	. . . .	1	6
8. EDWARD ARBER. **An Introductory Sketch to the 'Martin Marprelate' Controversy, 1588-1590**,	. . . . . .	3	0
9. [*Rev.* JOHN UDALL.] **A Demonstration of Discipline**,	. . . .	1	6
10. RICHARD STANIHURST. **'Æneid I.-IV.'** in English hexameters,	. . . .	3	0
11 **'The Epistle,'**	. . . .	1	6
12. ROBERT GREEN. **Menaphon**,	. . . .	1	6
13. GEORGE JOY. **An Apology to William Tyndale**,		1	6
14. RICHARD BARNFIELD. **Poems**,	. . . .	3	0
15. *Bp.* THOMAS COOPER. **An Admonition to the People of England**,	. . . . .	3	0
16. *Captain* JOHN SMITH. **Works.** 1120 pages. Six Facsimile Maps. 2 Vols.,	. . . .	12	6

1. William Caxton,
our first Printer.

Translation of REYNARD THE FOX.
1481.

[COLOPHON.] *I haue not added ne mynusshed but haue folowed as nyghe as I can my copye which was in dutche / and by me* WILLIAM CAXTON *translated in to this rude and symple englyssh in th[e] abbey of westmestre.*

Interesting for its own sake; but especially as being translated as well as printed by CAXTON, who finished the printing on 6 June 1481. The Story is the History of the Three fraudulent Escapes of the Fox from punishment, the record of the Defeat of Justice by flattering lips and dishonourable deeds. It also shows the struggle between the power of Words and the power of Blows, a conflict between Mind and Matter. It was necessary for the physically weak to have Eloquence: the blame of REYNARD is in the frightful misuse he makes of it.

The author says, "There is in the world much seed left of the Fox, which now over all groweth and cometh sore up, though they have no red beards."

2. John Knox,
the Scotch Reformer.

THE FIRST BLAST OF THE TRUMPET, &C.
1558.

(*a*) *The First Blast of the Trumpet against the monstrous Regiment of Women.*

(*b*) *The Propositions to be entreated in the Second* BLAST.

This work was wrung out of the heart of JOHN KNOX, while, at Dieppe, he heard of the martyr fires of England, and was anguished thereby. At that moment, the liberties of Great Britain, and therein the hopes of the whole World, lay in the laps of four women —MARY of Loraine, the Regent of Scotland; her daughter MARY (the Queen of Scots); Queen MARY TUDOR; and the Princess ELIZABETH.
The Volume was printed at Geneva.

(*c*) KNOX'S *apologetical Defence of his* FIRST BLAST, &C. *to Queen* ELIZABETH.
1559.

3. Clement Robinson,
and divers others.

A HANDFUL OF PLEASANT DELIGHTS.
1584.

A Handefull of pleasant delites, Containing sundrie new Sonets and delectable Histories, in diuers kindes of Meeter. Newly deuised to the newest tunes that are now in vse, to be sung: euerie Sonet orderly pointed to his proper Tune. With new additions of certain Songs, to verie late deuised Notes, not commonly knowen, nor vsed heretofore.

OPHELIA quotes from *A Nosegaie &c.* in this Poetical Miscellany; of which only one copy is now known.
It also contains the earliest text extant of the *Ladie Greensleeues*, which first appeared four years previously.
This is the Third printed Poetical Miscellany in our language.

4.
[Simon Fish,
of Gray's Inn.]

A Supplication for the Beggars.
[? 1529.]

A Supplicacyon for the Beggars.

Stated by J. Fox to have been distributed in the streets of London on Candlemas Day [2 Feb. 1529].

This is the Fifth Protestant book (not being a portion of Holy Scripture) that was printed in the English Language.

The authorship of this anonymous tract, is fixed by a passage in Sir T. More's *Apology*, of 1533, quoted in the Introduction.

5.
[Rev. John Udall,
Minister at Kingston on Thames.]

Diotrephes.
[1588.]

The state of the Church of Englande, laid open in a conference betweene Diotrephes *a Byshopp,* Tertullus *a Papiste,* Demetrius *an vsurer,* Pandochus *an Innekeeper, and* Paule *a preacher of the word of God.*

This is the forerunning tract of the *MARTIN MARPRELATE Controversy*. For the production of it, Robert Waldegrave, the printer, was ruined; and so became available for the printing of the Martinist invectives.

The scene of the Dialogue is in Pandochus's Inn, which is in a posting-town on the high road from London to Edinburgh.

6.
[?]

The Return from Parnassus.
[Acted 1602.] 1606.

The Returne from Pernassus: or The Scourge of Simony. Publiquely acted by the Students in Saint Iohns Colledge in Cambridge.

This play, written by a University man in December 1601, brings William Kemp and Richard Burbage on to the Stage, and makes them speak thus:

"Kemp. Few of the vniuersity pen plaies well, they smell too much of that writer *Ouid* and that writer *Metamorphosis*, and talke too much of *Proserpina* and *Iuppiter*. Why herees our fellow *Shakespeare* puts them all downe, I [Ay] and *Ben Ionson* too. O that *Ben Ionson* is a pestilent fellow, he brought vp *Horace* giuing the Poets a pill, but our fellow *Shakespeare* hath given him a purge that made him beray his credit:
"Burbage. It's a shrewd fellow indeed:"

What this controversy between Shakespeare and Jonson was, has not yet been cleared up. It was evidently recent, when (in Dec. 1601) this play was written.

7.
Thomas Decker,
the Dramatist.

THE SEVEN DEADLY SINS OF LONDON, &c.
1606.

The Seuen deadly Sinnes of London: drawn in seuen seuerall Coaches, through the seuen severall Gates of the Citie, bringing the Plague with them.

A prose allegorical Satire, giving a most vivid picture of London life, in October 1606.

The Seven Sins are—
   FRAUDULENT BANKRUPTCY.
   LYING.
   CANDLELIGHT (*Deeds of Darkness*).
   SLOTH.
   APISHNESS (*Changes of Fashion*).
   SHAVING (*Cheating*), and
   CRUELTY.

Their chariots, drivers, pages, attendants, and followers are all allegorically described.

8.
The Editor.

AN INTRODUCTORY SKETCH TO THE MARTIN MARPRELATE CONTROVERSY.
1588-1590.

(*a*) *The general Episcopal Administration, Censorship, &c.*
(*b*) *The Origin of the Controversy.*
(*c*) *Depositions and Examinations.*
(*d*) *State Documents.*
(*e*) *The Brief held by Sir* JOHN PUCKERING, *against the Martinists.*

The Rev. J. UDALL (who was however *not* a Martinist); Mrs. CRANE, of Molesey; R ev. J. PENRY; Sir R. KNIGHTLEY, of Fawsley, near Northampton; HUMFREY NEWMAN, the London cobler; JOHN HALES, Esq. of Coventry; Mr. and Mrs. WEEKSTON, of Wolston; JOB THROCKMORTON, Esq.; HENRY SHARPE, bookbinder of Northampton, and the four printers.

(*f*) *Miscellaneous Information.*
(*g*) *Who were the Writers who wrote under the name of* MARTIN MARPRELATE?

9.
[Rev John Udall,
Minister at Kingston on Thames.]

A DEMONSTRATION OF DISCIPLINE.
1588.

A Demonstration of the trueth of that discipline which CHRISTE *hath prescribed in his worde for the gouernement of his Church, in all times and places, vntill the ende of the worlde.*

Printed with the secret Martinist press, at East Molesey, near Hampton Court, in July 1588; and secretly distributed with the *Epitome* in the following November. For this Work, UDALL lingered to death in prison.

It is perhaps the most complete argument, in our language, for Presbyterian Puritanism, as it was then understood. Its author asserted for it, the infallibility of a Divine Logic; but two generations had not passed away, before (under the teachings of Experience) much of this Church Polity had been discarded.

10.
Richard Stanyhurst,
the Irish Historian.

Translation of
ÆNEID I-IV.
1582.

Thee first fovre Bookes of VIRGIL *his Æneis translated intoo English heroical [i.e.,* hexameter] *verse by* RICHARD STANYHURST, *wyth oother Poëtical diuises theretoo annexed. Imprinted at Leiden in Holland by* IOHN PATES, *Anno M. D. LXXXII.*

This is one of the oddest and most grotesque books in the English language; and having been printed in Flanders, the original Edition is of *extreme* rarity.

The present text is, by the kindness of Lord ASHBURNHAM and S. CHRISTIE-MILLER, Esq., reprinted from the only two copies known, neither of which is quite perfect. GABRIEL HARVEY desired to be epitaphed, *The Inventor of the English Hexameter*; and STANYHURST, in imitating him, went further than anyone else in maltreating English words to suit the exigencies of Classical feet.

11.
Martin Marprelate.

THE EPISTLE.
1588.

Oh read ouer D. JOHN BRIDGES, *for it is a worthy worke: Or an epitome of the fyrste Booke of that right worshipfull volume, written against the Puritanes, in the defence of the noble cleargie, by as worshipfull a prieste,* JOHN BRIDGES, *Presbyter, Priest or Elder, doctor of Diuillitie, and Deane of Sarum.*

The Epitome [*p.* 26] *is not yet published, but it shall be, when the Byshops are at conuenient leysure to view the same. In the meane time, let them be content with this learned Epistle.*

Printed oversea, in Europe, within two furlongs of a Bounsing Priest, at the cost and charges of M. MARPRELATE, *gentleman.*

12.
Robert Greene, M.A.

MENAPHON.
1589.

MENAPHON. CAMILLAS *alarum to slumbering* EUPHUES, *in his melancholie Cell at Silexedra. VVherein are deciphered the variable effects of Fortune, the wonders of Loue, the triumphes of inconstant Time. Displaying in sundrie conceipted passions (figured in a continuate Historie) the Trophees that Vertue carrieth triumphant, maugre the wrath of Enuie, or the resolution of Fortune.*

One of GREENE'S novels, with TOM NASH'S Preface, so important in reference to the earlier *HAMLET,* before SHAKESPEARE'S tragedy.

GREENE'S "love pamphlets" were the most popular Works of Fiction in England, up to the appearance of Sir P. SIDNEY'S *Arcadia* in 1590.

13.
George Joy,
an early Protestant Reformer.

AN APOLOGY TO TINDALE.
1535.

An Apologye made by GEORGE JOYE to satisfye (if it may be) W. TINDALE: to pourge and defende himself ageinst so many sclaunderouse lyes fayned vpon him in TINDALS vncharitable and vnsober Pystle so well worthye to be prefixed for the Reader to induce him into the vnderstanding of hys new Testament, diligently corrected and printed in the yeare of our Lorde 1534, in Nouember [Antwerp, 27 Feb. 1535.]

This almost lost book is our only authority in respect to the surreptitious editions of the English *New Testament*, which were printed for the English market with very many errors, by Antwerp printers who knew not English, in the interval between TINDALE'S first editions in 1526, and his revised Text (above referred to) in 1534.

14.
Richard Barnfield,
of Darlaston, Staffordshire.

POEMS.
1594-1598.

The affectionate Shepheard. Containing the Complaint of DAPHNIS *for the Loue of* GANYMEDE.

In the following Work, BARNFIELD states that this is "an imitation of *Virgill*, in the second Eglogue of *Alexis*."

CYNTHIA. *With Certaine Sonnets, and the Legend of* CASSANDRA. 1595.

The Author thus concludes his Preface: "Thus, hoping you will beare with my rude conceit of *Cynthia* (if for no other cause, yet, for that it is the First Imitation of the verse of that excellent Poet, Maister *Spencer*, in his *Fayrie Queene*), I leaue you to the reading of that, which I so much desire may breed your Delight."

The Encomion of Lady PECUNIA*: or, The praise of Money.* 1598.

Two of the Poems in this Text have been wrongly attributed to SHAKESPEARE. The disproof is given in the Introduction.

15.
T[homas] C[ooper].
[Bishop of WINCHESTER.*]*

ADMONITION TO THE PEOPLE OF ENGLAND.
[1589.]

An admonition to the people of England: VVherein are ansvvered, not onely the slaunderous vntruethes, reprochfully vttered by MARTIN the Libeller, but also many other Crimes by some of his broode, objected generally against all Bishops, and the chiefe of the Cleargie, purposely to deface and discredite the present state of the Church.
[*Jan.* 1589.]

This is the official reply on the part of the Hierarchy, to MARTIN MARPRELATE'S *Epistle of* [Nov.] 1508: see No. 11 on *p.* 24.
It was published between the appearance of the *Epistle* and that of the *Epitome*.

16.
Captain John Smith,
President of Virginia, and Admiral of New England.

WORKS.—1608-1631.

A complete edition, with six facsimile plates.

Occasion was taken, in the preparation of this Edition, dispassionately to test the Author's statements. The result is perfectly satisfactory. The Lincolnshire Captain is to be implicitly believed in all that he relates of his own personal knowledge.

The following are the chief Texts in this Volume:—

(1.) **A true Relation of Occurences in Virginia.** 1608.
(2.) **A Map of Virginia.** 1612.
(3.) **A Description of New England.** 1616.
(4.) **New England's Trials.** 1620 and 1622.
(5.) **The History of Virginia, New England, and Bermuda.** 1624.
(6.) **An Accidence for young Seamen.** 1626.
(7.) **His true Travels, Adventures, and Observations.** 1630.
(8.) **Advertisements for Planters in New England, or anywhere.** 1631.

The first Three English Books on America. [? 1511]-1555.

This Work is a perfect Encyclopædia respecting the earliest Spanish and English Voyages to America.

Small Paper Edition, 456 pp., in One Volume, Demy 4to, £1, 1s.
Large Paper Edition, in One Volume, Royal 4to, £3, 3s.

The Three Books are—

(1.) **Of the new landes, etc.** Printed at Antwerp about **1511**. *This is the first English book in which the word* America [*i.e.*, Armonica] *occurs.*
(2.) **A Treatise of the new India, etc.** Translated by RICHARD EDEN from SEBASTIAN MUENSTER'S *Cosmography:* and printed in **1553**. *The Second English Book on America.*
(3.) **The Decades of the New World, etc.,** by PIETRO MARTIRE [PETRUS MARTYR], translated by RICHARD EDEN, and printed in **1555**. *The Third English Book on America.* SHAKESPEARE obtained the character of CALIBAN from this Work.

A List of 837 London Publishers, 1553-1640.

This Master Key to English Bibliography for the period also gives the approximate period that each Publisher was in business.

Demy, 4to, 32 pp., 10s. 6d. net.

Fcap. 4to, Cloth, Gilt, 10s. 6d. *net.*

THE ONLY KNOWN FRAGMENT OF

The First printed English New Testament, in Quarto.

By W. TINDALE and W. ROY.

Sixty photo-lithographed pages; preceded by a critical PREFACE.

BRIEFLY told, the story of this profoundly interesting work is as follows:—

In 1524 TINDALE went from London to Hamburg; where remaining for about a year, he journeyed on to Cologne; and there, assisted by WILLIAM ROY, subsequently the author of the satire on WOLSEY, *Rede me and be nott wrothe* [see *p.* 19], he began this first edition in 4to, *with glosses*, of the English New Testament.

A virulent enemy of the Reformation, COCHLÆUS, at that time an exile in Cologne; learnt, through giving wine to the printer's men, that P. QUENTAL the printer had in hand a secret edition of three thousand copies of the English New Testament. In great alarm, he informed HERMAN RINCK, a Senator of the city, who moved the Senate to stop the printing; but COCHLÆUS could neither obtain a sight of the Translators, nor a sheet of the impression.

TINDALE and ROY fled with the printed sheets up the Rhine to Worms; and there completing this edition, produced also another in 8vo, *without glosses*. Both editions were probably in England by March 1526.

Of the six thousand copies of which they together were composed, there remain but this fragment of the First commenced edition, in 4to; and of the Second Edition, in 8vo, one complete copy in the Library of the Baptist College at Bristol, and an imperfect one in that of St. Paul's Cathedral, London.

In the *Preface,* the original documents are given intact, in connection with *Evidence connected with the first Two Editions of the English New Testament, viz., in Quarto and Octavo*—

I. WILLIAM TINDALE'S antecedent career.
II. The Printing at Cologne.
III. The Printing at Worms.
IV. WILLIAM ROY'S connection with these Editions.
V. The landing and distribution in England.
VI. The persecution in England.

Typographical and Literary Evidence connected with the present Fragment—

I. It was printed for TINDALE by PETER QUENTAL at Cologne, before 1526.
II. It is not a portion of the separate Gospel of *Matthew* printed previous to that year.
III. It is therefore certainly a fragment of the Quarto.

Is the Quarto a translation of LUTHER'S *German Version?*

Text. The prologge. Inner Marginal References. Outer Marginal Glosses.

⁎⁎⁎ For a continuation of this Story see G. JOY'S *Apology,* at *p.* 25.

Captain WILLIAM SIBORNE.

The Waterloo Campaign. 1815.

4th Ed.   Crown 8vo.   832 *pages.*   13 *Medallion Portraits of Generals.*   15 *Maps and Plans.*

Bound in Red Cloth, uncut edges.   FIVE SHILLINGS, Net.

The Work is universally regarded to be the best general Account in the English language of the Twenty Days War: including the Battles of Quatre Bras, Ligny, Waterloo, and Wavre; and the subsequent daring March on Paris. It is as fair to the French as it is to the Allies.

WILLIAM BEATTY, M.D., Surgeon of H.M.S. Victory.

An Authentic Narrative of the Death of Lord Nelson.

21st October 1805.

2nd Ed.   Crown 8vo.   96 *pages.*   *Two Illustrations:*

(1) Of Lord **NELSON** in the dress he wore when he received his mortal wound.

(2) Of the Bullet that killed him.

Bound in Blue Cloth, uncut edges.   HALF-A-CROWN, Net.

Other volumes in preparation.

3 *Vols. Fcap. 8vo, Cloth,* £1, 1s.

The Paston Letters.

1422-1509.

A NEW EDITION, containing upwards of 400 letters, etc., hitherto unpublished.

EDITED BY

JAMES GAIRDNER,

of the Public Record Office.

3 *Vols. Fcap. 8vo, Cloth extra,* 15s. *net.*

' *The Paston Letters* are an important testimony to the progressive condition of Society, and come in as a precious link in the chain of moral history of England, which they alone in this period supply. They stand, indeed, singly, as far as I know, in Europe; for though it is highly probable that in the archives of Italian families, if not In France or Germany, a series of merely private letters equally ancient may be concealed; I do not recollect that any have been published. They are all written in the reigns of HENRY VI. and EDWARD IV., except a few that extend as far as HENRY VII., by different members of a wealthy and respectable, but not noble, family; and are, therefore, pictures of the life of the English gentry of that age.'—HENRY HALLAM, *Introduction to the Literature of Europe,* i. 228, Ed. 1837.

These Letters are the genuine correspondence of a family in Norfolk during the Wars of the Roses. As such, they are altogether unique in character; yet the language is not so antiquated as to present any serious difficulty to the modern reader. The topics of the letters relate partly to the private affairs of the family, and partly to the stirring events of the time: and the correspondence includes State papers, love letters, bailiff's accounts, sentimental poems, jocular epistles, etc.

Besides the public news of the day, such as the Loss of Normandy by the English; the indictment, and subsequent murder at sea of the Duke of SUFFOLK; and all the fluctuations of the great struggle of YORK and LANCASTER; we have the story of JOHN PASTON'S first introduction to his wife; incidental notices of severe domestic discipline, in which his sister frequently had her head broken; letters from Dame ELIZABETH BREWS, a match-making Mamma, who reminds the youngest JOHN PASTON that Friday is 'Saint Valentine's Day,' and invites him to come and visit her family from the Thursday evening till the Monday, etc., etc.

Every Letter has been exhaustively annotated; and a Chronological Table with most copious Indices, conclude the Work.

MESSRS. A. CONSTABLE AND COMPANY'S
COMPLETE CATALOGUE

CONTAINING

THE WHITEHALL SHAKESPEARE
(*Large type in handy volumes*).

CONSTABLE's Reprint of the Author's Favourite Edition of the
WAVERLEY NOVELS
in 48 Vols.

THE ACME LIBRARY
Etc.

Will be sent post free on application.

www.ingramcontent.com/pod-product-compliance
Lightning Source LLC
Chambersburg PA
CBHW032242080426
42735CB00008B/969